THE FIRST AGE

OF THE PORTUGUESE EMBASSIES,
NAVIGATIONS AND PEREGRINATIONS
IN PERSIA (1507-1524)

BY

RONALD BISHOP SMITH

Printed by
DECATUR PRESS, INC.
BETHESDA, MARYLAND
1970

AUTHORS FROM WHICH THIS BOOK IS COMPOSED

1. Albuquerque, Braz de 1500-1580
2. Amatus Lusitanus 1511-1568
3. Barros, João de 1496-1570
4. Castanheda, Fernão Lopes de .... d. 1559
5. Correa, Gaspar .... d. 1560s
6. Couto, Diogo de 1542-1616
7. Ferreira, Miguel (apud Gaspar Correa) .... fl. 1509-1540s
8. Goes, Damião de 1502-1574
9. Herbert, Thomas 1606-1682
10. Monardes, Niculoso de .... ca. 1512-1588
11. Orta, Garcia da .... d. 1568
12. Ramusio, Giovanni Battista 1485-1557
13. Silva y Figueroa, Don Garcia de 1550-1624
14. Simões, Gil .... fl. 1515-1516
15. Tenreiro, Antonio .... fl. 1523-1565
16. Valle, Pietro della 1586-1652

3

PREFACE

"Who is so worthless or indolent as not to wish to know by what means and under what system of polity the Romans in less than fifty-three years have succeeded in subjecting nearly the whole inhabited world to their sole government" Polybius asks his readers in the introduction to his history. I, with more reason, ask my readers, *who* is so worthless or idle as not to wish to know something of the manner whereby Christian Europe introduced itself to Asia? *Who* is so worthless as not to wish to know how the Portuguese entered the Kingdom of Persia—a kingdom so illustrious in antiquity. And *who* is so worthless or idle as to wish to remain entirely ignorant of what routes, in what circumstances, and in what manner the Portuguese journeyed to the court of Persia at Tabriz? Surely it would be a great shame for anyone to plead guilty to my query, since the expansion of Rome in antiquity and the expansion of the Western world are the two supreme events in the secular history of Western civilization. In Europe the expansion of Rome terminated in the triumph of the Christian religion. The result of Western expansion is not yet comprehended. Moreover the sphere of action of Western civilization is not Europe alone, but the entire world, and now the universe beyond. Since the dignity of a faculty, as a mental discipline, is known by its object and extension, with great reason then we should desire to inform ourselves of the first age of Western expansion in Asia. Polybius in the Second Century B.C. was fully conscious of the greatness of his subject, and I would be remiss if I were not fully alive to the dignity of mine.

My desire, my ambition these past five years has been to write the First Age of the Portuguese entry into Asia—because the Portuguese led the way—and because during this time I have come to like many things of Portuguese life—utilizing all known sources for my work, learning whatever languages, visiting whatever places, reducing the particulars of that first age to a system, attempting to delineate and to illustrate the initial Portuguese itineraries to the courts of Asia, attempting what has never been attempted. This is my desire, my purpose and my ambition. I hope to sow a plant from which the reader will gather much fruit and flower.

In preparing this volume of the Portuguese Embassies, Navigations and Peregrinations, the third I have published, I have continually meditated the criticism that Polybius directed against Timaeus, a historian who confessed to know only documents and memoirs as the sources of his history, and not the places of which he wrote, and seeking to avoid a like censure in me, I asked Vasco Vieira Garin, Portuguese Ambassador to the United States, if he could help me secure a sum of money to enable me to unite my research in Lisbon with a visit to Persia to view some of the places visited by the Portuguese ambassadors in the first quarter of the sixteenth century. And with his prompt and attentive assistance, and by favor of the Fundação Calouste Gulbenkian of Lisbon, I was awarded a grant of money adequate to meet my expenses for a visit to Persia, during May of 1970, in which I saw many of the places visited by the Portuguese, not the least being the extensive Plain of Marvdasht upon which the ruins of Persepolis are situated, and the cities of Tehran, Saveh, Qom, Isfahan and

Shiraz. I was particularly anxious to visit Persia, because I know a little of the written language, and because the Portuguese sources are more detailed with regard to Portuguese routes of entry in Persia than for the other parts of Asia of a like period, thus enabling me to trace the itinerary of two of the three principal Portuguese embassies in great detail.

Among the many things I had occasion to notice during this voyage is the very striking similarity which Iranian women bear to Portuguese women, both as to their physical appearance and in the manner in which they carry themselves, being with greater circumspection and decorum than the women of America and Northern Europe, who in recent years have become frivolous, vain and immodest to the last degree. Tacitus should see his Germans now! Pray would he cry or laugh? This close resemblance greatly surprised me, although my Portuguese sources, for the period of which I write, constantly reiterate the Persians, removing the differences of religion and civilization, are the same people as the Portuguese, such a great impression did they make upon the Portuguese of the sixteenth century. In my opinion, however, the resemblance between the male Portuguese and Persian is not very great. The Persian women differ from the ladies of Lisboa in this, that they cover themselves when they go abroad with a light semi-transparent veil which falls to the foot, and which they wrap around themselves, hiding all but the face, and some women are so particular in hiding their features from the glances of men, they raise the veil with their finger to cover the mouth leaving only their forehead, eyes and nose exposed, and thus I saw them walk the streets of Isfahan. These usages and others I noted in a report which I wrote in Portuguese to the Fundação Calouste Gulbenkian of my itinerary in Iran, and I do not speak more of them, but rather of what I consider a great defect in Oriental studies.

The great sin of Orientalists has been (and will continue to be) their lack of knowledge of the Portuguese language, which they refuse to learn out of ignorance of the worth of Portuguese literature and contempt for the Portuguese, a vast mistake, and as the Portuguese lack such facilities as the Library of Congress and the British Museum, in which to supplement their researches, and are only partially aware of the great advances which have been made in Oriental studies, it is not surprising no one has yet attempted to apply the Moslem literature to illustrate and annotate the Portuguese entry into Persia. Those Orientalists who have never read João de Barros, Fernão Lopes de Castanheda, Antonio Tenreiro or Gil Simões, and those Portuguese who are unfamiliar with Khvand Amir, Hasan-i-Rumlu, Hamd-Allah Mustawfi and the *Fars Namah* are not very well placed to write of the Portuguese entry into Persia. Khvand Amir and Hasan-i-Rumlu are not the historians of the calibre of João de Barros and Fernão Lopes de Castanheda, nor are any of the Persian histories mentioned by Ghulam Sarwar, *History of Shah Isma'il Safawi*, Aligarh, 1939 (in his bibliography) to be compared in accuracy, depth or grandeur of purpose with the illustrious Barros or Castanheda. Still a knowledge of the works of the Persian historians, contemporary, or nearly contemporary with the arrival of the Portuguese in Iran, is necessary for the study of the embassies of Miguel Ferreira (1514-1515), Fernão Gomes de Lemos (1515-1516) and Balthasar Pessoa (1523-1524), and I think

6

I can claim that I am a pioneer in these studies, being the first to apply the Moslem sources to the study of the Portuguese entry into Persia. With reference to the embassy of Miguel Ferreira, however, I have attempted little, because I have not determined whether Miguel Ferreira arrived at the court of Iran before or after the Battle of Chaldiran (where Turkish artillery overthrew the Persian cavalry on August 23rd 1514). Since the primary source for the embassy of Miguel Ferreira is lost, I am per force dependent on Gaspar Correa, the worst of sources, and Correa appears to indicate Miguel Ferreira arrived at court before August 23rd 1514, but this is by no means established. If it is ascertained when Miguel Ferreira arrived at court, before or after Chaldiran, it is possible to assign Persian names to those Portuguese titles given the Persian officials that M. Ferreira met at court, and this by means of literature discovered in certain journals of distinguished oriental societies centered at London, Paris and Leiden. At a later date perhaps I shall attempt to identify these persons when I am in possession of more certain intelligence. But if not, I think whatever Portuguese, if curious, may answer some of these questions himself by means of the literature which I intend to bring to Lisbon and offer to the Biblioteca da Academia das Ciências de Lisboa.

RONALD BISHOP SMITH

POTOMAC, MARYLAND

AUGUST 31, 1970

PART I

THE PORTUGUESE EMBASSIES, NAVIGATIONS AND VISITS

CHAPTER I

TENTATIVE CONTACTS OF THE PORTUGUESE WITH THE KINGDOM OF PERSIA

The Medieval Kingdom of Ormuz dominated the commerce of the Persian Gulf and the Iranian hinterland. The city-state of Ormuz, like the Kingdom of Malacca (of equal fame and obscurity), grew rich, powerful and fat by reason of trade, and lying as they did, and still do, athwart important lines of communication, at different and opposite ends of the Indian Ocean, location gave to Ormuz and Malacca a special advantage.

The wealth and fame of Ormuz attracted the Portuguese like the lodestone attracts iron, and the iron of the Portugals wrought for Ormuz, as it wrought for Malacca, a yoke which Afonso de Albuquerque applied to one as to the other, harnessing Ormuz and Malacca to that Portuguese imperial van of state which he drove with such fierce ardor, and apparent reckless abandon, during the term of his governorship of India (1509-1515). We eschew the conquest of Ormuz, and the circumstances which brought the Portugals to Ormuz; in this volume we take these for granted, in all but superficial purview, as we took for granted the Portuguese conquest of Malacca in our volume of the Portuguese embassies to Southeast Asia. Our narrative will carry us to the Medieval Kingdom of Persia, and though Ormuz is today a part of the Modern Kingdom of Iran, it is but a desolate rock in the Persian sea, no longer an independent kingdom, an albatross scarcely known amongst the princes and lands of the present generation. We shall not be tempted by the wealth of Ormuz. It is no more.

In the year 1506 King Manuel I (1495-1521) of Portugal dispatched a great fleet of fourteen, fifteen or sixteen vessels to India commanded by Tristão da Cunha for the purpose of erecting a fortress on the island of Socotra, situated at the entrance of the Gulf of Aden, and to nourish the Portuguese possessions in India with men and materials. Beneath his command Tristão da Cunha carried a smaller squadron captained by Afonso de Albuquerque: the king having ordered the latter to cruise upon the Arabian coast in search of prizes. The Portugals of the conserve of Tristão da Cunha and Afonso de Albuquerque, visited the coast of East Africa with fire and sword, explored part of the island of Madagascar, expelled the Moors of Fartak from Socotra, and established a Portuguese fortress on the island in 1507.

These things entertained, and accomplished, Afonso de Albuquerque sailed from Socotra on or about August 20th of 1507 with seven ships and four hundred sixty men: captains, besides himself, Francisco de Tavora, Manuel Teles, Afonso Lopes da Costa, Antonio do Campo and João da Nova, all captains of *naos*, and Nuno Vaz de Castelo Branco, captain of a *fusta*. Tristão da Cunha had already sailed for India on August 10th 1507 (or possibly somewhat earlier).

8

Albuquerque resolved to navigate for Ormuz, and to conquer it, judging the king of Portugal might best be served by adding that wealthy kingdom to his growing Asian seigniory. Albuquerque and armada wrought havoc on the coasts of Oman, reducing the ports en route, which were tributary to the Kingdom of Ormuz, either to ashes, or to the obedience of the Portuguese crown. Like another Gideon the terrible Afonso de Albuquerque smote Oman with his mighty sword and delivered the land from the hand of Midian and the Amalekites.

EXTRACT OF THE LETTER OF AFONSO DE ALBUQUERQUE TO THE VICEROY
OF INDIA DOM FRANCISCO DE ALMEIDA
Dated Ormuz, 2nd February 1508

"God gave to me such a good wind and voyage [sailing from Socotra], that I arrived upon the city of Calaiate [Kalhat] and by force I obliged it to render and give many provisions without repayment, and by [the] bad counsels of [the] captains, I did not lay my hands [on it], and it remained obedient to the King our lord. And from that place I departed and went upon the town of Curiate [Qaryat] and I fought it and I delivered it by force of arms and put it all to the sword. At that place I loaded provisions, allowing the people to sack everything else, so that they made great profit. From that place I raised anchor and went upon the town of Mazcate [Muscat] and I fought it and I entered it by force of arms, putting all to the sword and setting it afire. Here I took many provisions and the people great wealth. From this place I raised anchor and went upon the town and fortress of Çoar [Suhar], and I determined to place [the] great artillery on land and to combat it. They did not dare to await the onset of battle, and all came to be placed in my hands. . . . And from there I raised anchor and went upon the town of Guorfaçaom [Khawr Fakkan] and I entered [it] by force of arms and followed the flight of the enemy for more than a league from the place, and I killed many people and set the town on fire.

"Thereafter I went upon the city of Ormuz and I anchored close by their very great armada of many people, and at another day, being noon time, I ordered the anchor of my *nao* raised with the armed *batés*, and I appeared in the middle of their armada and thus I ordered the several captains to do it, and they did it. I fought with it, and I fought and destroyed many people and I placed their *naos* on the bottom, in which many people drowned. I burned the suburb and as many *naos* as there were in land. They placed themselves in my hands, and I took from them fifteen thousand xarafins of tribute and five thousand for the expenses of [the] armada."

(*Cartas de Affonso de Albuquerque*, Tomo I, Carta II 1508-Fevereiro 2   Letter of Afonso de Albuquerque to Dom Francisco de Almeida—Ormuz)

The Portuguese, having introduced themselves to the proximity of Persia in this manner, waged a sanguinary warfare against the forces of the Kingdom of Ormuz, evident in the prose of Afonso de Albuquerque, who reduced the kingdom to a temporary bondage. But a new war with Ormuz was not long igniting—the reason: four men of the Portuguese conserve had fled to the city and Coge Atar (Khwaja Attar), the king's first minister and principal man of the kingdom, refused to surrender the fugitives at Albuquerque's beck and command. Albuquerque, therefore, desired vengeance. The captains considered the new war equally unjust and unnecessary, and three of them, Manuel Teles, Afonso Lopes da Costa and Antonio do Campo, willingly risked the displeasure of Afonso de Albuquerque and King Manuel I by absconding to India in protest with their ships. The Great Afonso was therefore obliged to effect a very mortifying retreat, consisting of his own retirement from Ormuz to Socotra, leaving the fortress of Ormuz unfinished and his conquest incomplete. Coming against Ormuz from the island of Socotra in September 1508, the Great Afonso de Albuquerque again found his forces insufficient to effect the decisive conquest he cogitated and he retired this time to India, having forced Ormuz to acknowledge a tributary status to the crown of Portugal, but wanting a fortress necessary to bring the island-state permanently within the Portuguese imperial system. The conquest of Ormuz remained incomplete until Afonso de Albuquerque, this time as governor of India, sailed to Ormuz in 1515, the year of his death. At that time Albuquerque had the forces, and the loyalty of his captains, and he fitted a yoke to Ormuz from which she never escaped.

Afonso de Albuquerque had sailed to Ormuz twice. The first visit lasted from September 1507 until February 1508 and his second from September 1508 until November of the same year. On both occasions the Portuguese laid hand on the Persian mainland since the operations of war had necessitated a search for provisions and the enemy, involving (on the second occasion) a brush with two captains of Shah Ismael on the coast of the *terra firme* opposite Ormuz. More importantly during the first voyage of Afonso de Albuquerque to Ormuz the Portuguese commenced to have relations with the Kingdom of Shah Ismael I (1502-1524).

In the days after Afonso de Albuquerque forced the king of Ormuz, and his first minister, Coge Atar, to agree to pay King Manuel of Portugal fifteen thousand xarafins of gold in tribute each year, and shortly after Albuquerque commenced to raise the fortress of Ormuz, which was in the month of October of 1507, he received word from Coge Atar, that, on the coast of the *terra firme* of Persia, opposite of Ormuz, two ambassadors of the king of Xiraz (Shiraz) had arrived asking for the tribute which the kings of Ormuz were wont to pay to the kings of Persia in the past. These ambassadors came on behalf of Shah Ismael of Persia—or Xeque Ismael as the sixteenth century Portuguese call him— the overlord of the king of Xiraz (Shiraz).* Coge Atar desired to know what reply to return to the ambassadors.

---

* João de Barros (Decada II Livro II Capitulo IV), Damião de Goes (Parte II Capitulo XXXIIII) and Additional MS 20901 of the British Museum (Capitulo 79) refer to two ambassadors with regard to this embassy. However, Braz de Albuquerque (Parte I Capitulo XXXVIII), Fernão Lopes de Castanheda (Livro II Capitolo LXIIII) and Gaspar Correa (Tomo I Capitulo VII) know of only one ambassador who Braz de Albuquerque, the son of Afonso, describes as

10

"Two honored men coming before him, Afonso de Albuquerque arranged to have an oath given to them on their Koran, delivering to them some balls of cast iron of [the] artillery, and some iron things from lances, and bundles of arrows, and he said, that by reason of the oath they had received, they would present those things to the Ambassadors, and they would say to them from the part of the Captain-major, that those Kings, and principal tributaries of the King of Portugal, his lord, when petitioned by another for some tribute, they paid it in that coin, because his arsenals of war were full for his enemies, and his treasury open for his friends if they had any need. And if the King of Xiraz [Shiraz] desired something else of King Ceifadim [Saif-ud-din] of Ormuz, that he Afonso de Albuquerque, remained there making a fortress which he would fill with that coin, and with very forceful and valiant *cavalleiros*, that he should petition that place for such payments, since they would reply for the King Ceifadim." (Barros, Decada II Livro II Capitulo IV)

It is strange that João de Barros, from whom we have quoted, in the very next sentence of his Decadas, or *Da Asia*, indicates this embassy was an invention of Coge Atar raised as a blind to deflect Afonso de Albuquerque from his purpose, which was to raise a fortress in Ormuz, judging I suppose, that by kicking this dust in his eye, Albuquerque might be intimidated. Barros, notwithstanding his intelligence to the contrary, is not corroborated by King Manuel, Braz de Albuquerque, Castanheda, Correa or Goes, all of whom note this embassy in essentially the same terms as Barros, and in no way indicate the Persian embassy to Afonso de Albuquerque was contrived, but that it was genuine, and that Afonso de Albuquerque replied to it in the strongest terms. Goes states the two ambassadors were scandalized by the reply, and Castanheda declares that the ambassador received the reply of Afonso de Albuquerque with great surprise and could not vouchsafe a reply.

Additional Manuscript 20901, Capitulo 79
Albuquerque, Parte I Capitulo XXXVIII
Barros, Decada II Livro II Capitulo I, Capitulo III & Capitulo IV
Castanheda, Livro II Capitolo LXIIII
Correa, Tomo I Capitulo VII—Terceiro Anno do Visorey Dom Francisco de Almeida
Goes, Parte II Capitulo XXXIIII

"a captain of Xeque Ismael accompanied by people on horseback." Neither Albuquerque, Castanheda or Correa associate the king of Shiraz with this embassy. Last but not least, King Manuel I, in a little known letter, noted in our Bibliography, declares thirty people came on horseback at this time, from the city of Cerache (undoubtedly Shiraz), asking for the customary tribute.

BIBLIOGRAPHY

PRINTED SOURCES

1. Albuquerque, Braz de. *Comentários do Grande Afonso de Albuquerque*, Imprensa da Universidade, Coimbra, 1923.
2. Barros, João de. *Da Asia*, Vol. 3, Lisbon, 1777.
3. Castanheda, Fernão Lopes de. *História do Descobrimento & Conquista da India pelos Portugueses*, Imprensa da Universidade, Coimbra, 1924.
4. Correa, Gaspar. *Lendas da India*, Lisbon, 1858.
5. Goes, Damião de. *Crónica do Felicissimo Rei D. Manuel*, Imprensa da Universidade, Coimbra, 1926.

PUBLISHED DOCUMENTS

1. *Carta de El-Rei D. Manoel para o Juiz, Vereadores e Procurador da Villa d'Elvas, dando Parte da tomada do Reino de Ormuz*, Imprensa da Universidade, Coimbra, 1908. Edition of Eugenio do Canto.
2. *Cartas de Affonso de Albuquerque*, Tomo I, Lisbon, 1884.
   a) Carta de Affonso de Albuquerque ao vice-rei—Ormuz, February 2, 1508: p. 9, 10. Carta II

MANUSCRIPTS

1. Additional Manuscript 20901 of the British Museum.

CHAPTER II

THE ABORTED EMBASSY OF RUY GOMES DE CARVALHOSA—1510

In the year 1510 a Persian ambassador accredited to the Sabaio of the Kingdom of Deccan (i.e. to King Yusuf Adil Shah, 1490-1510) arrived at Goa in February or March and discovered that the Sabaio had died and that Afonso de Albuquerque, the governor of India (1509-1515), had taken possession of Goa, the principal port of the Deccan. The ambassador variously Mirabuçaca, Mirabucaca or Mir Bubáca in the Portuguese sources (i.e. Mir Abu Ishak in modern transcription), decided to render his embassy to Afonso de Albuquerque, with the presents that he bore. João de Barros and the Additional MS 20901 of the British Museum record the ambassador fetched eighty horses from Ormuz to sell in Goa, and that twenty of these horses were purchased by the governor of India. Albuquerque the son declares the ambassador arrived a few days before Albuquerque the father conquered Goa for the first time. But the King Dom Manuel declares the ambassador arrived after the conquest.

EXTRACT OF THE LETTER OF KING DOM MANUEL TO THE BISHOP OF SEGOVIA

Dated Lisbon, 12th July 1511

". . . we have other letters from the said, our captain-major [Afonso de Albuquerque], by which he has informed us how arrived, being he in the said city of Goa, the ambassador of Xeque Ismael, called in those parts Sofy, who rules Persia, and about whom they speak [of his] great deeds, who came accredited to the king of the said city of Goa [to King Yusuf Adil Shah], bringing presents and messages for him, and finding our said captain-major in the said city, and, Our Lord be praised, possessed of all the kingdom of Goa, he related to him that he was dispatched by his lord to the king of Goa, and finding that we were king and lord of Goa, by your [our] said captain-major, he would present to him in our place the present and embassy that he brought. Our said captain-major sent to us the said present which is some horse coverings with very rich cloths for them, worked in very fancy needlework in gold and silk, and very rich cloths of silk of those wont to be found in those parts, and many rich *toucas*-turbans and other things, and a red *carapuça*-cap with a very high *trufa*-turban, of those which all the people of war of the said Xeque Ismael wear as a sign of who they are so as to be known in battles from the others. He offered friendship from the part of his king and lord to our said captain-major, and our said captain-major sent our person [i.e. Ruy Gomes de Carvalhosa] with him in order that we shall be more particularly informed of his power and of his things. Our said captain-major writes us that this Xeque Ismael besieged the Sultan [of Egypt] in the city of Leepo [Aleppo] which he says is a great city of his dominions, and which he put in great necessity, and that he also has continual war with the

Turk." (*Cartas de Affonso de Albuquerque*, Tomo III 1511-
Julho 12 Letter of the King of Portugal to the Bishop of
Segovia—Lisbon)

Both Braz de Albuquerque and Gaspar Correa relate the Persian ambassador, who came in company of another ambassador of Ormuz, after relating the
grandeur of the royal estate of the king, and his desire to be known to all parts,
requested two things of Afonso de Albuquerque. Firstly he desired the governor
of India, now that he was in possession of Goa, to force the Moslems of the
land to embrace the law of Xeque Ismael (i.e. to conform to the tenets of the
Shiah sect of the Moslem religion) and to oblige the Goans to pray by the books
of Xeque Ismael in their mosques. Secondly this ambassador of Shah Ismael
desired the governor to mint coinage in Goa bearing the insignia of Xeque
Ismael. The ambassador might have asked for the moon. Albuquerque consented
to neither demand with these reasons *a saber*: when the Moors surrendered Goa
to the Portuguese, he had granted them a royal *seguro* (to wit a royal license)
assuring the Moors of their religious liberty, and so much as to the coinage of
Xeque Ismael, the governor declared he was greatly surprised that the ambassador should ask such a thing, since all kings greatly esteem their insignias on their
coins as a sign of their dominion, and no king would freely suffer another monarch
to mint specie in his lands.

> "The ambassador responded to him that he had come to Goa
> with an embassy directed to the Çabaio [King Yusuf Adil
> Shah of Bijapur], and he carried those things in his instruc-
> tion for the purpose of speaking to him about them, and find-
> ing that he was dead, and his lordship in possession of the
> kingdom of Goa, and doing what he should, he said to him
> what Xeque Ismael his lord had ordered him, since he was
> his ambassador; and that if he had errored in this matter, then
> he asked for reward that he would pardon him, since the obli-
> gation of ambassadors was to guard their instructions, his
> being to make what suited the service of his king. Having
> finished this matter, the ambassador asked that he would dis-
> patch him, because he wished to depart." (Albuquerque, Parte
> II Capitulo XXIII)

Afonso de Albuquerque desired the ambassador to remain assured of his
friendly disposition towards him, that he desired to dispatch a messenger with
him, one Ruy Gomes de Carvalhosa, who, according to Braz de Albuquerque
and Gaspar Correa, the principal sources for this embassy, came to India in
the fleet of the Marshall of Portugal, Dom Fernando Coutinho, which sailed
from Lisbon in March of 1509 and arrived in India in October of the same
year. This Ruy Gomes, aver Albuquerque and Correa, came to India as an
exile (*degradado*) banished from the Kingdom of Portugal for some felicity
unknown to me. Albuquerque, the son, in his *Comentários do Grande Afonso
de Albuquerque*, and Albuquerque, the father, in a letter printed in the same
work, declare Ruy Gomes was a servant of the king (*criado delRey*). The apparent incongruity of these statements is not alleviated by our scrutiny of the Portu-

guese sources. Afonso de Albuquerque found Ruy Gomes a situation as Portuguese ambassador to the court of Persia. It cost Ruy Gomes de Carvalhosa his life.

By the instrumentality of his ambassador Afonso de Albuquerque wrote this letter to Shah Ismael of Persia, and another to the king of Ormuz, and gave his ambassador a *regimento* of those things he should accomplish.

THE LETTER OF AFONSO DE ALBUQUERQUE TO THE KING OF PERSIA CARRIED BY RUY GOMES AND FOUND IN PARTE II CAPITULO XXIII OF THE *COMENTARIOS DO GRANDE AFONSO DE ALBUQUERQUE*

"Very great and powerful lord amongst the Moors, Xeque Ismael: Afonso de Albuquerque captain-general and governor of India for the very high and very mighty the King D. Manuel, king of Portugal, and of the Algarves, on this side and on the other side of the sea, in Africa lord of Guinea, and of the conquest, navigation [and] commerce of Ethiopia, Arabia, Persia and of India, and of the kingdom and dominion of Ormuz, and of the kingdom and dominion of Goa. I give you to know, how I, gaining the city and kingdom of Goa, found in it your ambassador to whom I made great honor, and I treated [him] as the ambassador of a very great king and lord, and I scrutinized all your things, as if he had been sent to these parts for the King of Portugal; and because I am certain that the King D. Manuel, my lord, will be pleased to have knowledge, friendship and intercourse with you, he has dispatched this messenger, to whom you will give credit in all things that he will say to you from my part, because he is [a] *cavaleiro criado* of the King my lord, [a] man instructed in war, educated in the arms of our custom, and he will know how to give to you a very good account of all the things of the kingdoms of Portugal. You will know in what manner I gained the city and kingdom of Ormuz by order of the King my lord, and afterwards I worked to have knowledge of your state, power and command and I desired to send messengers to you if the things of Ormuz had not gone awry, the which I hope in God will soon be settled, because I await to go there in person, and from there I will work to see you on the coast of the sea and [at the] ports of your kingdoms because the power I bring of the King my lord, with ships and people at sea, is for the purpose of expelling and destroying the *náos* of the Sultan [of Egypt] which come to India and wish to establish themselves there, which deed with [the] help of God, we have finished, because his captain, Mirocem [Amir Husain], and his armada, were defeated at Diu, and they captured all his *náos* and artillery, and they killed all his people. And now I defeated them [the Moors favored by the Sultan of Egypt] and I conquered the city of Goa and all their armada, and I expelled them from it, as your ambassador will say to you; and because I understand that he is your enemy, and makes war to you, I send this news to you, and I offer my person, and armada, and

15

people of the King my lord to help you destroy him, and I will be against him every time that you desire me to be. And if you desire to destroy the Sultan by land, you will have great aid from [the] armada of the King my lord by sea, and I believe that with little labor you will be able to seize the city of Cairo and all his kingdom and lands, and thus the King my lord will be able to give you great aid by sea against the Turk, and his armadas by sea; and you with your great power, and people of horse by land, will make it very difficult for him to be able to defend himself. And in India he has great armadas by which to help you. Thus the friendship and favor of so powerful a king, as is the King my lord by sea and land, you should wish to have, and you should send your ambassadors to him, because he will be very pleased to see whoever knows how to give account of your kingdoms and dominions. And if God ordains that this friendship and commerce come to pass—come with your power upon the city of Cairo and the lands of the Great Sultan that march with you, and the King my lord will pass to Jerusalem, and you will gain all the land on that side: and for certainty with regard to what you expect to accomplish, it is desirable for you to send your messengers and by them you will have reply from the King my lord, and meanwhile I will be advised of what you wish me to do, or to what part the armada of the King my lord may go, so that it will make more damage to the Sultan in your service." *

By the embassy of Ruy Gomes de Carvalhosa the governor of India sought to introduce the Portugals to Shah Ismael I of Persia. But alas fate decreed against Afonso de Albuquerque. Having dispatched Ruy Gomes with Frade João, apparently as his interpreter (*lingoa*), and a servant, with Albuquerque's letter for the king of Persia, and another for the king of Ormuz, and in company with the Persian ambassador, the Portuguese embassy embarked from Goa for the voyage to Persia in two *náos*: captain "a honored Moor of Cananor" named Cogeamir (Khwaja Amir). By means of the said Cogeamir (Khwaja Amir) the governor of India wrote a letter to Cogeatar (Khwaja Atar), the first minister of the king of Ormuz, inviting him to return to the obedience of the king of Portugal. Albuquerque solicited the minister to pay the tribute in accordance with the obligations imposed upon him, and declared that the enmity of the past, which existed between them, should be forgotten. Moreover by this same letter Afonso de Albuquerque sought a boon from Cogeatar for the Persian ambassador, requesting that no duties be levied against his merchandise at Ormuz, and that moreover Cogeatar should work to bestow upon Ruy Gomes horses (*encavalgaduras*), money and all necessary things to facilitate his entry into Persia. Cogeatar was of no mind to either please or appease Afonso de

---

* This letter comes a little more complete, or a little more ornamented, but basically the same, in the anonymous Additional MS 20901 of the British Museum, Capitulo 95.

16

Albuquerque. After he had received Ruy Gomes with evidences of great affection and friendship, and questioned him about the conquest of Goa, and for Afonso de Albuquerque, sending the Portuguese ambassador to his lodgings, and promising that he would dispatch the ambassador promptly after he rested from his journey, Cogeatar had manner whereby he poisoned Ruy Gomes since he believed Afonso de Albuquerque was out of sorts with the king of Portugal and because he feared an alliance between the crowns of Persia and Portugal. He seized all the merchandise of the Persian ambassador and recouped his losses with insults. Frade João and the servant returned to India, having escaped with their lives, by what means we know not, nor do we know of what transpired with the Persian ambassador, although he reached Persia, and "Cogeamir," in the words of Braz de Albuquerque, "remained unloading his *náos,* and making his merchandise, and departed for India." In this sad manner terminated the first Portuguese attempt to establish relations with the court of King Ismael.

Additional Manuscript 20901, Capitulo 95
Albuquerque, Parte II Capitulo XXIII
Barros, Decada II Livro V Capitulo III
Castanheda, Livro III Capitolo CXLIII
Correa, Tomo II, Lenda de Afonso de Albuquerque, Capitulo IX & Capitulo X
Goes, Parte III Capitulo IIII; Parte IV Capitulo IX

BIBLIOGRAPHY

PRINTED SOURCES

1. Albuquerque, Braz de. *Comentários do Grande Afonso de Albuquerque,* Imprensa da Universidade, Coimbra, 1923.
2. Barros, João de. *Da Asia,* Vol. 3, Lisbon, 1777.
3. Castanheda, Fernão Lopes de. *História do Descobrimento & Conquista da India pelos Portugueses,* Imprensa da Universidade, Coimbra, 1928.
4. Correa, Gaspar. *Lendas da India,* Lisbon, 1860.
5. Goes, Damião de. *Crónica do Felicissimo Rei D. Manuel,* Imprensa da Universidade, Coimbra, 1926.

PUBLISHED DOCUMENTS

1. *Cartas de Affonso de Albuquerque,* Tomo II, Lisbon, 1898.
    a) Regimento que Affonso de Albuquerque deu a Ruy Gomes e a frei João quando os mandou a Narsinga [alas Persia] ao Xeque Ismael— March[?] 1510: p. 79-83.
2. *Cartas de Affonso de Albuquerque,* Tomo III, Lisbon, 1903.
    a) Carta del-rei D. Manuel ao bispo de Segovia, em que lhe dá parte da tomada de Goa e da embaixada do Xeque Ismael—Lisbon, July 12, 1511: p. 20, 21.

MANUSCRIPTS

1. Additional Manuscript 20901 of the British Museum.

CHAPTER III

THE EMBASSY OF MIGUEL FERREIRA—1513-1515

Shah Ismael, the First of that name, established the Shiah sect of the religion of Muhammad as the national religion of Persia. The first king of the Safavid dynasty unified Persia after nine hundred years of division and foreign rule, and made Tabriz his capital in 1502. From Tabriz, in the region of Azerbaijan, whence his ancestors had sprung, Shah Ismael conquered Persia (1502-1508) and parts of Turkey and Irak as well. Many historians view Shah Ismael I (1502-1524) as the founder of Modern Persia. We might hold with equal justice, that, although he unified the realm of Persia, he did not free that ancient kingdom from the fetters of foreign rule, as he, and most of his officers of state were Turks, speaking a language more foreign to Persian than either English or Portuguese. It is not our office to judge Shah Ismael, whether he should, or should not be considered as merely another conqueror of a people, long oppressed, who were a nation when the English and Portuguese had yet to be differentiated from the tribe of Germans and the empire of the Romans. Having established the Shiah religion in Persia, Shah Ismael, in testimony of the ardour of his faith, was wont to proselytize in foreign parts.

EXTRACT OF A LETTER OF AFONSO DE ALBUQUERQUE TO DUARTE GALVAM

Undated, but written in 1514

"In the year past two ambassadors of Xeque Ismael entered India: one in the Kingdom of Cambay and the other in the Kingdom of Deccan, each one with one hundred *emcavalguaduras*-horses, [each ambassador] dressed in silk and brocade, swords worked in silver and gold, and a great store of baggage, [and] their tents in fine clothwork (*antretalhadas*) and very rich, and silver for the service of their table. The purport of their embassies was that they would receive his *carapuça*-cap and book of his oration. They were well received and poorly dispatched. The one who came to the Kingdom of Deccan arranged to visit me [by means of his messenger] bringing cloths of silk and brocade. He did not find me there [i.e. in Goa] since I had already departed for the Red Sea, and there he left the present that he brought for me. What I knew in Goa by him was that Xeque Ismael had been informed how I had dispatched messengers and message to him, and [that] they were taken at Ormuz, which has now recently received the *carapuça* and sect of Xeque Ismael, and it grieves me very much, because if Ormuz should fall into his hands, it will be very difficult to regain it, and I do not wish to see such a great lord placed in India, even if he is our friend."
(*Cartas de Affonso de Albuquerque*, Tomo I, Carta CVIII Letter of Afonso de Albuquerque to Duarte Galvão)

18

Dated Cananor, 4th December 1513

"Arriving at Goa [from the Red Sea] I found a present of
cloths of Persia and a ring with a diamond, which the ambassador of Xeque Ismael sent to me, who came to the King
of Deccan [Mahmud, 1482-1518] and to the son of the
Çabayo [King Ismael Adil Shah, 1510-1534], and some offerings from [the] part of Xeque Ismael, and they returned to
where the ambassador was, when they did not find me, and
they left the said things; that, coming I from the Red Sea,
the ambassador would come to see and speak to me upon the
things of Xeque Ismael, before his departure for Persia."
(*Cartas de Affonso de Albuquerque*, Tomo I, Carta XLI
1513-Dezembro 4   Letter of Afonso de Albuquerque to the
King—Cananor)

In the fall of 1513, Afonso de Albuquerque, after his return voyage from
the Red Sea to Goa, sailed to Malabar, to concert the affairs of the Portuguese
fortresses and factories in that part of India, where discord was rife, and which
merited the undivided attention of the governor of India, and a *strong* will.
Having arrived at the port of the city-state of Cananor, Afonso de Albuquerque
received the Persian messenger of the ambassador of Xeque Ismael, who, having
come to Goa once again from the Deccan, since he understood the governor had
returned from the Red Sea, and knowing at Goa that Afonso de Albuquerque had
sailed to Cananor, he proceeded to that port in search of him. This messenger
bears the title and name of Coge Alijão in the *História do Descobrimento &
Conquista da India pelos Portugueses* of Fernão Lopes de Castanheda (Livro III
Capitolo CXXXVIII), Cojealeam in the *Crónica do Felicissimo Rei D. Manuel*
of Damião de Goes (Parte III Capitulo LXVII) and Bairim Bonari in the *Da
Asia* of João de Barros (Decada II Livro X Capitulo II & Capitulo V). The
messenger gave his message to Afonso de Albuquerque, in Castanheda to know,
that the ambassador of Xeque Ismael, knowing the great things that Albuquerque
had accomplished in India, greatly desired to see the governor, but as he could
not come, he dispatched his messenger—and offered friendship to the governor.
The substance of the message, according to Braz de Albuquerque, was to ask
Albuquerque for a *seguro* for his passage to Ormuz, and more importantly, for
the purposes of our history, the messenger requested the governor of India to
dispatch a Portugal to proceed in company of the Persian embassy to the court of
Persia. Castanheda declares the governor, perceiving in the messenger a desire
to view the grandeur of the Portuguese estate, showed him the Portuguese
fortresses at Cananor and Calicut, and from the latter city-state carried the messenger to Cochin where he dispatched the Persian envoy with a present and
Miguel Ferreira, a native of Beja (avers João de Barros), with a letter for the
king of Persia: and the same *regimento* that Ruy Gomes de Carvalhosa carried:

19

offering the king of Persia in his name felicitations, an alliance, and the friendship of the Portuguese.*

Miguel Ferreira, in a party of five Portuguese, including João Ferreira, his relation, and second ambassador of the embassy, and João Caldeira as the interpreter—and with four slaves, of whatever race or denomination, I know not—departed from Cochin in mid-December of 1513. To Gaspar Correa we owe the knowledge of the composition of the Portuguese embassy, and Correa gathers his intelligence, not from imagination and faulty investigation, as so often, but from the best of sources, a notebook (*caderno*) of remembrances of Miguel Ferreira, which Gaspar Correa declares he had in his possession (*o qual caderno eu houve a meu poder*), and which is now irretrievably lost. And from Braz de Albuquerque, and from two *mandados* (or letters of command) described in the Bibliography, we ascertain the approximate date of departure of Miguel Ferreira from Cochin, who passed to Goa, in company of the Persian messenger, and then to either Chaul or Dabul, or perhaps to both, and thence from India sailed to Ormuz in company of the Persian ambassador, who joined his messenger at Dabul or Chaul, and brought in his company an ambassador of the Hidalcão (i.e. King of Bijapur).†

---

* It is well to notice some of the discrepancies among the Portuguese sources with reference to the embassy of the Persian "messenger." João de Barros (Decada II Livro X Capitulo II) indicates the messenger came to Goa, to meet the governor there, and from that citadel of Portuguese power, Albuquerque carried him to Cananor. But the intelligence of Barros appears to be wanting in truth, or verisimilitude, as we gage by weighing the justice of his remarks with a perusal of the histories of Albuquerque, Castanheda, Correa and Goes, or by an exacting study of the *Cartas de Affonso de Albuquerque*, Lisbon, 1884-1935. Gaspar Correa declares, and at some length (Tomo II Capitulo XLIII), that the Persian ambassador himself came to visit Albuquerque, not in Malabar, but at the port of Chaul, before the return of Afonso de Albuquerque to Goa from the Red Sea. Alas Gaspar Correa has wandered far from the high road of truth, and to judge by the carriage of his remarks, he was either ill, or in some other manner indisposed, when he inscribed his particulars of the Persian ambassador, in the *Lendas da India*, so misshapen is his intelligence, as to suggest a torpor of the brain, arising from an excessive, or toxic, vapor of the stomach, powerfully affecting his reason. We shall present Gaspar Correa in a better light (we hope) when we relate the particulars of the itinerary of Miguel Ferreira in the Kingdom of Persia, since Gaspar Correa, alone amongst the sixteenth century Portuguese historians, has noticed the embassy of Miguel Ferreira in any detail, and that from the most primary of sources, a *caderno*-notebook of Miguel Ferreira.

† Barros (Decada II Livro X Capitulo II) and Correa (Tomo II Capitulo XLVIII) declare Miguel Ferreira and the Persian embassy sailed from Chaul, but Braz de Albuquerque (Parte IV Capitulo XVII & Capitulo XIX) declares they sailed from Dabul.

"Miguel Ferreira departed from Chaul in a *nao*, in company with the ambassador of Xequesmael [Sheikh or Shah Ismael] and another of the Hidalcão [King Ismael Adil Shah of Bijapur], and they all sailed to Ormuz where they were well befriended by the King, and from there they passed to the *terra firme*, called Mogostão [Mughistan], where the ambassador of the Hidalcão remained sick, and they proceeded on their way on camels since horses are not of service because the land is full of crags. On these camels they carry some *ceirões*-great containers made of *verga*-rods, in which they are settled, and they sleep when they wish, with awnings for protection against the sun, and there they carry their water and *mantimento*-provisions. And proceeding upon their journey they found great places and villages, [having] houses of *barro*-mud covered with thatch. In some places there are castles of stone, low walls, weak things. The lands are wasted since the lords are tyrants, and these lords are often replaced since no one has patrimony. Xequesmael gives his commanders lands for their upkeep, only so much as it pleases him, to each one according to the people of arms that he has. The lands are well supplied with wild animals, and game, and birds of many varieties. It has very cold regions with great snows, little firewood [and] it is destitute of *mantimentos*-provisions. Their principal *mantimento* consists of dates since there are many palm trees in the valleys and very little rice. Wherever they arrived the captain [of their camel train] sent a message ahead, saying that he carried a Portuguese that his lord had sent to fetch in India. This message being given to the lord of the land, they came to receive them along the way with their people and they were lodged in the best houses of the place, and they were accustomed to make service of things to eat. They travelled after the sun arose, until it set, by reason of the great cold. The captain paid all the expenses.

"Thus proceeding in this manner, Miguel Ferreira sent to whip one, his slave, who, because of this, searched for poison and he gave it to him in order to kill him. He [Miguel Ferreira] finding himself with poison, the captain made great diligence with many remedies; nevertheless he was near death, so that they were detained for three months during which time they did not travel and the captain had great works for his health, and he weeped, saying his lord would behead him because of his illness. Miguel Ferreira gave great assurances to him.

"Xequesmael had great pleasure knowing that Miguel Ferreira came, and seeing that he delayed, he sent to know the reason, and the reply coming that the delay was occasioned because of illness, Xequesmael ordered that he be carried placed in a litter, and that should he die, then he would kill them all. Then he was placed in a litter lined with skins inside and outside, with cloths, and felts, and hides, so that it was very close and hot going his way, and without any air, which litter men carried from place to place. In this manner they travelled until they arrived near a city called Xiraz [Shiraz*], where they said Xequesmael was, and being eight leagues from the city, a lord of that land came his way, who went to war with his people, which were five thousand armed men on horseback, in front of whom proceeded an array of people on foot, that were ten thousand men, and another array of ten thousand men on horseback with their captains, instruments [and] flags. All these armed people, chiefly the [men on] the horses, [that] were caparisoned and concerted in very good order, came near the way that Miguel Ferreira proceeded, who was already well from his infirmity, and in the litter he was exposed to view." (Correa, Tomo II Capitulo XLVIII)

From Gaspar Correa we relate the salient particulars of the embassy of Miguel Ferreira, and Gaspar Correa with the *caderno* of Miguel Ferreira in his possession, understood that the captain (*capitão*) of the army which had crossed the path of Miguel Ferreira, approaching the Portuguese ambassador, raised the lance he bore and thrust it into the ground, whereupon the people of his conserve fell silent, and coming alone before Miguel Ferreira, spoke to him, and offered to accompany the ambassador to the king. Miguel Ferreira thanked the captain, accepted his offer, and with the pomp of war proceeded in a body with the captain that day towards the king of Persia. The captain of the camel train related to Miguel Ferreira that this captain of men-at-arms was continually at

---

* From Ormuz Braz de Albuquerque declares Miguel Ferreira and his embassy "made their way straight to Tauriz [Tabriz], where Xeque Ismael was, who was already advised of the coming of Miguel Ferreira by a letter of his ambassador, and also by means of the ambassador of the Hidalcão, who went in their company." (Albuquerque, Parte IV Capitulo XIX) Unfortunately, beyond this brief statement, Braz de Albuquerque has not noticed the particulars of the ambassador's itinerary, while Gaspar Correa, with the *caderno* of Miguel Ferreira before him, notices the itinerary of the Portuguese ambassador in great detail, although he, like Braz de Albuquerque, and all the Portuguese sources, is deficient in dates and place names, so that we are unable to follow the track of this embassy, unlike the embassies of Fernão Gomes de Lemos (1515) and Balthasar Pessoa (1523-1524), whose itineraries we shall note in Chapters VI and X. From a close scrutiny of the full text of Gaspar Correa, I suspect he meant to say Tabriz, not Shiraz, since Correa indicates Miguel Ferreira has arrived at the court of Persia, which in Shah Ismael's reign (1502-1524) was situated at Tabriz, although of course, it is not only probable, but quite likely, that Miguel Ferreira and conserve en route to the capital of Persia, passed through the city of Shiraz.

22

war, and that he had lands with which to pay his people, and that Xequesmael, the king of Persia, had twenty captains of the purport of the captain with whom the ambassador had conversed, all with as many people, and these captains, not having war, were always at court with the king, and that this other captain had been commanded by the king to give account of himself.

That day, after a journey of seven leagues, Miguel Ferreira took his lodgings one league from Xiraz (Shiraz); so avers Gaspar Correa, but we opine Tabriz, for the reasons we expounded in the last footnote. This night Xequesmael came to visit the ambassador and asked for his health. The ambassador responded that he asked God for health so that he might have the corporeal forces to see such a mighty and celebrated prince as the king of Persia. This reply pleased the king and he dispatched his personal physician (*fisico mór*) to attend to what remained of the infirmity of Miguel Ferreira.

Gaspar Correa describes this *fisico mór* as the chief lord of the kingdom, who had won his spurs by curing a painful defect in the king's ear, which the king had contracted as a youth of few years, and which had tormented the royal person for many years. And the king, after many doctors and masters of medicine had been put to death for their inability to effect a cure, out of gratitude to this physician for his proficiency in the medical art, and successful treatment of Shah Ismael, made him a great man of state and the principal lord of the kingdom.

"The next day (*Ao outro dia*) Miguel Ferreira proceeded to Xiraz [alas Tabriz] where the King was, and along the way the *fisiqo*-physician came to see him by order of the King, accompanied by five hundred [men] of horse, and with him the *gozil mór*-bailiff-major of the King. The *fisiqo* had the cloth of the litter raised, and saw the face of Miguel Ferreira, and he covered the litter, and he said to the *gozil* that he had been given poison, and the *gozil* immediately gave orders to fetch the captain who came with Miguel Ferreira, and arranged to behead him, and his servants went to cry before Miguel Ferreira saying that they wished to kill their lord. Miguel Ferreira raised the cloth, and shouted that they should give the captain to him and not to make evil to him; and thus it was done. Arriving at the city, which was very great and with beautiful houses, by order of the *fisiquo*, Miguel Ferreira was placed in some houses that were as hot as houses of bath, which did not admit any air, only light through the window-panes, so that one could see what went on on the outside, and he did not see the *fisiqo* again, who only sent remedies from the apothecary's to him, and a man had care of him, while he and his servants were not obliged to pay for anything. And presently finding himself well again, the King sent to give him two thousand xarafins for his expenses. And because he was now well, they provided him with very good houses in a garden which had [a] great orchard of many fruits and trees, where Miguel Ferreira thoroughly enjoyed himself, and never departed for the outside since by *regimento* he was forbidden to do so, and in his condition he had pleasure to remain in [the] house forever. And he had a white slave of his, [a] gentle and very well dressed man, who was his *lingoa*-interpreter since he knew how to speak Persian very well.[*] The king ordered beautiful female musicians to sing and dance inside the house, and they spoke and jested with Miguel Ferreira freely; but he dispatched them with gifts and courteous words, without ever to understand with them, because with regard to this he had been strictly instructed in his *regimento* and because he was very honest in his mode of living.

"Having a month that Miguel Ferreira had now recovered his perfect health, the King sent for him to come to the palace, since he also desired other ambassadors from different parts to come [to the palace]. The said day arriving, Miguel Ferreira was very well dressed in [a] jerkin of red satin, and his sword of gold and [a] dagger, and [a] *gorra*-cap of crimson velvet with [a] rich print and [a] white feather and [an] upper garment of the same red satin, and leggings of crimson satin and slippers lined with satin, and this, because he was obliged to go barefoot on the carpets of the *estrado*-estrade of the King; and his servants were dressed in *grā*-scarlet-ingrain, lined with green velvet, with their *gorras*-caps and gilded swords; and the *lingoa*, who would do the talking, wore a jerkin of yellow damask and his leggings and *gorra*.

"And in the afternoon of the day that he had to proceed to the King, the *fisico mór*-chief physician and the *gozil*-bailiff came for him, and he went between them and other lords, with many people on horseback; and from the King came a horse caparisoned with gold and silver; and there they joined other ambassadors who Xequesmael had ordered to go with him, who he did not wish to hear until that time. The said ambassadors went after Miguel Ferreira,[†] and arriving at the palaces they came to a great patio of paved white stones, of twice the greatness of the Recio [Rossio] of Lisbon,[‡]

---

* In a different part of the *Lendas da India* (Tomo II Capitulo XLIII) Gaspar Correa declares João Caldeira, who bears a Portuguese name, was entrusted with the office of *lingoa*. The *lingoa*, here described by Correa as a slave of Miguel Ferreira, ought to be a different person than João Caldeira.

† Among the ambassadors in the procession of Miguel Ferreira was the ambassador of the Hidalcão (i.e. the ambassador of the king of Bijapur) "greatly aggravated" by the deference shown to Miguel Ferreira by the king on this occasion. (Albuquerque, Parte IV Capitulo XIX)

‡ If we except the Praça do Comercio, the Rossio is the great square of modern Lisbon, located half a mile inland from the former, and effectively the center of modern Lisbon.

24

entirely surrounded by great houses of the King with great varandas, windows, sentry-boxes, painted and carved towers of masonry, and gilded *curucheos*-spires, so that they appeared to be the houses of [a] great King. The patio was full of armed people who appeared to be ten thousand.

"They ascended to a great *sala*-chamber full of noble people, and the upper part of the *sala* had beautiful paintings in gold and silver, and they passed to another *sala* on the same floor, likewise richly painted above and along the walls, in which *sala* there was a carpet covering the entire floor. No one entered this *casa*-room save ambassadors and the great lords who preceded Miguel Ferreira. Thus all made their courtesies in this *casa*, placing their hands upon the face, and lowering the head as far as the floor; and returning, they were placed toward the sides [of the room], and the *físico*-physician and *gozil*-bailiff went forward with Miguel Ferreira in [the] middle, because beyond this *casa* was still another, and Xequesmael was in another beyond [it], so that all the doors were opened one after the other, and the King was seated in front of the [last] door looking at the ambassadors. And arriving at the door of this *casa*, which was [the] ante-chamber of that where the King was, the *regedor*-governor of the Kingdom came from inside, and took Miguel Ferreira by the hand and placed him in the ante-chamber by himself, so that no other person entered with him, whence entering, he made his reverence with the knee touching the floor, which was carpeted and furnished with velvet and brocade, and the *regedores* and principal officials of the Kingdom and of the house of the King were placed along the walls; the youthful *lingoa* remained at the door. Xequesmael was seated on a *banca*-bench covered with a cloth of gold, and there was little light within the *casa*. At the door of this chamber was the *regedor* who spoke. Miguel Ferreira was on his feet, and the youth, who would do the speaking, on his knees close by him. The King ordered Miguel Ferreira to sit upon a carpet laid on another carpet which covered the entire *casa*. Miguel Ferreira made another great courtesy, and settled with one knee on the floor, and the King sent that he would settle to his will. Miguel Ferreira returned to make another courtesy, and sat down. The King then spoke with the *regedor*, and the *regedor* with Miguel Ferreira, and he asked about his health. He responded that he was in perfect health since he saw with his own eyes his royal person, so that he remained greater and more honored than so many men [who] came from Portugal to India. Then he unwrapped a letter from a [piece of] linen, taking it in the hand, and he raised it as high as he could, and *regedor* took it and carried it to the King, and he opened a door or window inside [the room], and the *casa*-room re-

25

mained brighter, and the person of the King and the *casa* more clearly seen, so that they glittered in gold. And the King dispatched Miguel Ferreira, and the door was shut, and Miguel Ferreira returned to the *gozil* and *fisiquo*—fetching him with their honors—and they carried him to other very noble *casas*-houses that were close by a great square. Xequesmael remained very content with the great notices which the Governor [of India] gave to him in his letter. At a later day (*Ao outro dia*) an overseer of his revenues (*védor da fazenda*), with many people on horseback, carried Miguel Ferreira for the city and showed it to him, which was four times the size of Evora, with [a] noble *casaria*-range of houses and great squares and houses of the great lords, and [the *casaria* was] entirely besieged by high walls and towers, and beyond this another enclosure with walls and towers, and beyond this another wall without towers, in such a manner that there were three enclosures, and from one to the other [there was so much] space that all the people of the city could fit into it, and converted gates, with back sides having great towers, with guards at them continually; there were more than forty gates.

"The King had four residences of his person with rich palaces in this city. The *vedor da fazenda* gave him a man who was always in his house and he was obliged to go to the city with his youths to buy all necessary things, for which this man paid, without Miguel Ferreira paying for a thing. He was continually visited by the captain with whom he had come from India, who instructed him upon all the things he should do, and that he should do whatever the King ordered, and to refuse nothing.

"The King desired Miguel Ferreira to sleep with [a] woman so that he would leave [a] son or daughter behind. He dispatched a white and very beautiful woman of his house, with rich jewels and cloths, and two female servants with her; and he declared it appeared to him to be a bad thing for a man not to have a woman; for this reason he dispatched that woman, who was [a] woman of his house, and she would serve him in all matters to his will. Miguel Ferreira returned great thanks and courtesies, asking him very circumspectly not to send her to him, because he was married in Portugal, and when he had departed, he had made an oath and had promised never to touch another woman until he returned, asking many pardons for not doing what His Highness had commanded. The King considered his virtue commendable." * (Correa, Tomo II Capitulo XLVIII)

---

* Miguel Ferreira's virtue (in this matter) is more suited to his mouth than his parts. Cf. the *Da Asia* of Diogo de Couto, Decada V Livro V Capitulo VIII,

Miguel Ferreira resided for a space of two months at this city, that we identify with Tabriz, and not with Shiraz, preferring the intelligence of Braz de Albuquerque, although he scarcely notices the embassy of Miguel Ferreira, to that of Gaspar Correa, even with his *caderno* of the Portuguese ambassador; since Correa in some manner has gone astray; because his description is that of Tabriz, the capital of Persia in the reign of Shah Ismael I (1502-1524), and certainly not that of Shiraz, which city the Portuguese sources aver had fallen into decay; and Gil Simões the scrivener of the embassy of Fernão Gomes de Lemos, of whom we shall speak in Chapter VI declares in his itinerary of that embassy, that the population of Shiraz consisted of three thousand and five hundred inhabitants, while the same Gil Simões declares the city of Tabriz consisted of sixteen thousand hearths, or a population, which we may estimate at seventy-five thousand souls, which agrees well with Correa's statement that the population was four times that of the Portuguese city of Evora, whose population in the first decades of the sixteenth century may be estimated at ten to twenty thousand people.

With the arrival of summer of this year 1514, Shah Ismael departed Tabriz for the hunt to which he was greatly addicted (as we gather from both Persian and Portuguese sources) and Gaspar Correa, per force as we have indicated, virtually the only source for the embassy of Miguel Ferreira, declares the king proceeded to this hunt seated in a litter carried on the shoulders of men, which, being lined with gold and precious stones, and possessed of a chair, was covered by a cloth as a protection against the sun. The king's majesty was fittingly displayed in his attire of long white *camisas*-shirts, a rich *cabaia*-Turkish tunic, a white *touquinha*-turban and a dagger ornamented in gold and precious stones at the waist. Behind the king came the *regedor* (literally the governor i.e. the *vakil* of the Persian sources), and behind the *regedor* one hundred caparisoned horses, and behind them the *estribeiro mór*-chief master of the horses.

The king ordered Miguel Ferreira to proceed in his company, and with the Portuguese ambassador, his *lingoa*, and as the king of Persia proceeded to the hunting field, the *regedor* and Miguel Ferreira conversed, and the former questioned the latter about the "things of Portugal."

Thus the royal procession arrived at the field which had been chosen for the hunt. Here the *caçador mór* (the officer charged with the organization of the hunt) distributed the people around a field enclosing a space of more than two and one half leagues diameter. The king meanwhile proceeded to the center of the field and stationed himself at the foot of a great tree which contained a *casinha*-small house like structure, from which one could view the entire field, and in which the king apparently placed himself to view the commencement of the hunt. With the king were a select company of men with birds of all kinds, including falcons of great size and beauty, and also *lebréos*-harriers, *galgos*-greyhounds and *onças caçadoras*-hunting leopards, and Miguel Ferreira with a lance which the Shah Ismael had given him so he could participate in the sport.

---

where Miguel Ferreira is found without wife, but with bastard sons, the illicit offspring of a long Indian residence. Likewise G. Schurhammer and E. A. Voretzsch *Ceylon zur Zeit des Königs Bhuvaneka Bahu und Franz Xavers 1539-1552*, Band I, Leipzig, 1928, p. 81, for the biography of said Miguel Ferreira.

On this day the hunt began, and Miguel Ferreira, a humble man of the West, who had left his family and native land, to sail to India for reasons unknown to the ken of history, witnessed a spectacle no modern man has ever seen, a hunt of the barbaric East on a scale worthy of Genghis Khan, with all the dimensions of a veritable war of man against beast. For at the proper time the Persian host encircling the field on the outside commenced to blow horns, to beat the bush and to shout—while moving toward the center of the field— forcing the animals from the circumference of the circle, toward the center, where the king, his men and Miguel Ferreira awaited. The animals, forced to enter an ever contracting area, were seized with fear, and ran from one side of the field to the other looking for an exit to escape the wrath of the hunters who goaded them from all sides. The game, which included stags, gazelle, wild pigs, and many other species of animals, in wild disorder came pell-mell to the center, and the king of Persia, at the propitious moment, unleashed his dogs and hunting leopards, who rushed at the game, fought with the enemy and returned with their prey to the king.

This mode of combat enduring for a period of time, the king ordered the hunters upon the rim of the circle to retreat a space in order to allow the game more freedom to maneuver, and as the animals commenced to flee the center for the circumference, the horsemen of Persia fell upon the disordered foe at the run with both lance, and bow and arrow, and killing and disabling the game, the nobles of Persia consummated a great massacre that day. The king passed from this field to another later in the day, and continued to hunt with *onças*-leopards that were carried on the backside of the horses. "The said animals when they perceived the game which the hunters could not see, leaped to the ground, and with the body very low, hiding themselves so the game could not see them, being near, with one leap they conquered the prey, and tearing it to pieces, they drink the blood, and then each one returns to his proper hunter." (Correa, Tomo II Capitulo XLVIII) Arriving at some great lakes (*humas grandes alagoas*), the king discovered numerous large and small birds of many varieties. At these lakes the king "made [a] great hunt" and returned to the city, being greeted by his courtiers along the way who awaited his return, and arriving at the city that evening, Shah Ismael brought more than ten thousand people in his company, and the city "had so many lamps in the windows that night became day," and taking leave of Miguel Ferreira at his palaces, the king dispatched the Portuguese ambassador to his house with many people to escort him.

"Then, a few days later, the King dispatched Miguel Ferreira with a great lord of his to see some of the things of his Kingdom in which he spent the entire summer, and they showed him many things, too many to account. And he went to the Kingdom of Armenia, which is separate [and] by itself, where he saw great beauty in men and women; where he saw a great church in masonry of great workmanship, and on the inside many paintings of gold, in [the] middle of which was, upon many *degraos*-steps enclosed by silver railings, a monument open at all the sides, lined with [a] sheet of gold and having a quantity of *pedraria*-precious stones,

28

and at the openings [were] some panes of crystal so that one could see what was on the inside, which was a body in bones. And Miguel Ferreira questioned for this thing, and they related to him that the body was of a holy man, who had made that house and many others throughout Armenia, and when he was alive he had made miracles, according to [what] they have in his legend, which according to presumption should be Saint Bartholomew, from what was found in the legend of Saint Thomas. . . . And Miguel Ferreira after seeing many things, returned to the King, and asked that he would dispatch him, because he had very great desire to relate to the Governor and people in India, such great things that he had seen. The King took much satisfaction with this, and presently dispatched him with [a] reward of five thousand xarafins, and rich presents, and he sent with him his ambassador, who had a great present to give him. Although Miguel Ferreira related many other things, and daily he inscribed them, I wrote these things, which appeared to me to be sufficient." (Correa, Tomo II Capitulo XLVIII)

Miguel Ferreira, his people, and the Persian ambassador in his company, the same messenger who came to Malabar to search for Afonso de Albuquerque, mentioned earlier in this chapter, arrived at Ormuz by a route the Portuguese sources have not sought to divulge—early in 1515; and preparing to depart for India, Afonso de Albuquerque, the governor of India, arrived at the Kingdom of Ormuz with a great fleet to construct the desired fortress, which in the course of this year he did construct, thereby completing the conquest of Ormuz which Albuquerque first essayed in 1507, and again in 1508, fully incorporating the Kingdom of Ormuz into the Portuguese imperial system. After noting the voyage of Pero de Albuquerque into the Persian Gulf, we shall return to Afonso de Albuquerque at Ormuz, and the embassy that he dispatched to Shah Ismael in the person of Fernão Gomes de Lemos.

Albuquerque, Parte IV Capitulo XII, Capitulo XVII, Capitulo XVIII & Capitulo XIX
Barros, Decada II Livro VII Capitulo III; Livro X Capitulo II & Capitulo V
Castanheda, Livro III Capitolo CXVII, Capitolo CXXXVI & Capitolo CXXXVIII
Correa, Tomo II, Lenda de Afonso de Albuquerque, Capitulo XLIII, Capitulo XLVII & Capitulo XLVIII
Goes, Parte III Capitulo LXVII

BIBLIOGRAPHY

PRINTED SOURCES

1. Albuquerque, Braz de. *Comentários do Grande Afonso de Albuquerque*, Imprensa da Universidade, Coimbra, 1923.
2. Barros, João de. *Da Asia*, Vol. 4, Lisbon, 1777.
3. Castanheda, Fernão Lopes de. *História do Descobrimento & Conquista da India pelos Portugueses*, Imprensa da Universidade, Coimbra, 1928.

4. Correa, Gaspar. *Lendas da India*, Lisbon, 1860.

5. Goes, Damião de. *Crónica do Felicissimo Rei D. Manuel*, Imprensa da Universidade, Coimbra, 1926.

6. [Simões, Gil]. *Do caminho que fizeram e do que passaram os embaixadores que foram ao Xeque Ismael, e o presente que leauaram, e da reposta que trouxeram.* Published in the *Cartas de Affonso de Albuquerque*, Tomo II, Lisbon, 1898.

PUBLISHED DOCUMENTS

1. *Cartas de Affonso de Albuquerque*, Tomo I, Lisbon, 1884.
   a) Carta de Affonso de Albuquerque ao rei—Cananor, October 19, 1510: p. 24. Carta VII
   b) Carta de Affonso de Albuquerque ao rei—Cananor, December 4, 1513: p. 242, 243. Carta XLI
   c) Carta de Afonso de Albuquerque a Duarte Galvão—Without date: p. 398. Carta CVIII

2. *Cartas de Affonso de Albuquerque*, Tomo II, Lisbon, 1898.
   a) Regimento que Affonso de Albuquerque deu a Ruy Gomes e a frei João quando os mandou a Narsinga [alas Persia] ao Xeque Ismael—March[?] 1510: p. 79-83.
   b) Instrumento de Affonso de Albuquerque para Manuel da Costa, feitor de Ormuz, pagar a Joham Machado o mantimento de todo o tempo que amdou em caminho do Xequesmaell [in the embassy of Miguel Ferreira], feito em Nazare davante de Ormuz a onze de Abril, Gaspar Correa o fez de 1515: p. 142. Strangely, Gaspar Correa has not otherwise noticed the participation of João Machado in the embassy of Miguel Ferreira.

3. *Cartas de Afonso de Albuquerque*, Tomo VII, Lisbon, 1935.
   a) Instrumento de Pero Mazcarenhas, capitão de Goa, para Francisco Corbinell, feitor de Goa, dar ao bramene embaixador do Çabayo e ao embaixador do Xeque Ismaell a cada huum sessemta pardaos em ouro—Goa, March 2, 1513: p. 73. Documento CXXXI
   b) Instrumento de Dom Garcia [de Noronha] para Alvaro Lopez, almoxarife dos mantimentos, dar dous barys de vinho ao meyxyjeyro do embaixador de Xaquesmael—Cochin, December 10, 1513: p. 102. Documento CXCIII
   c) Instrumento de Pero Mazcarenhas para Francisco Corvinel dar a Manoel de Sampayo dous pardaos e meo que deu de manteiga e gallinhas ao embaixador do chequesmaell em Pamgym—Goa, December 17, 1513: p. 104. Documento CXCVII

MANUSCRIPTS

1. Codice 50-V-21 of the Biblioteca da Ajuda, Lisbon.

CHAPTER IV

THE VOYAGE OF PERO DE ALBUQUERQUE TO THE ISLAND OF BAHRAIN AND THE PERSIAN GULF—1514

In the month of February of 1514 the governor of India, Afonso de Albuquerque, dispatched his nephew, Pero de Albuquerque, with an armada of four *naos* to the mouth of the Red Sea to make prizes of the many Moslem *naos* sailing the seas of Arabia. The governor of India instructed Pero de Albuquerque by *regimento*, to wit, coming the winter, or the wet monsoon (which in the Indian Ocean commences in April-May), he should proceed to Ormuz to collect the tribute owed to the crown of Portugal, being two years outstanding, and to ask leave to complete the fortress that Albuquerque had commenced, and to have a factory site. Moreover Pero de Albuquerque received instructions to enter the Persian Gulf and to discover the island of Bahrain. Pero de Albuquerque carried in his conserve four *naos*, captains beside himself, Ruy Galvão de Menezes, Jeronymo de Sousa and Antonio Raposo de Beja. With this powerful engine of plunder Albuquerque sailed to Socotra, where he fetched water, and thence to the mouth of the Red Sea, where he captured ten *naos* of the Moors, and with the winter approaching, Pero de Albuquerque departed for Ormuz in accordance with the *regimento* that he carried, and with his prizes, arriving at Ormuz in May. Having dispatched Tristão de Ga to the king of Ormuz, Torunxá (Turan Shah), who succeeded Ceifadim (Saif-ud-din), who had been murdered, to petition on the matter of the fortress and tribute, and receiving an unsatisfactory reply, Pero de Albuquerque determined to discover Bahrain, and leaving Tristão de Ga and João Teixeira as factors to sell his merchandise (or more appropriately, his plunder), and Christovão Cercado and Vasco Pires as their scriveners, Pero de Albuquerque sailed from Ormuz with two pilots given to him by the king of Ormuz.

> "And with this, he departed [Ormuz] on July 7th of the said year [of 1514], and he entered by the strait of the sea of Persia, and discovered all the ports, islands and places in it, as far as an island called Lulutem [Halul?*]. And being as far ahead as Bárem [Bahrain], since the winds were from the west, and delayed his return to India, as he had been instructed in his *regimento*, he turned around, [and] being two days from it, he came to Raxel [Rishahr], where he found Mirbuzaca [Mirabuçaqua in Castanheda, Livro III Capitolo CXXVIII and Mir Bubac in Barros, Decada II Livro X Capitulo I], [a] captain of Xeque Ismael, who had taken twenty *terradas* from a captain of the king of Ormuz. When Pero de Albuquerque knew of this, he communicated with him, saying that the great Afonso de Albuquerque had dispatched him to those parts with that armada in service of the king of Ormuz, and he asked him for reward, that he would deliver

---

* Lulutem is probably the modern island of Halul: Albert Kammerer, *La Mer Rouge l'Abyssinie et l'Arabie depuis l'Antiquité*, Tome Deuxième, Parte I, Cairo, 1935, p. 206. Lulu, in Arabic, means pearl.

the *terradas* which he had taken from his captain. Mirbuzaca as he did not possess [an] armada by which to resist ours, delivered the *terradas* to him, and everything else which he had taken. And after the captain had delivered them, Pero de Albuquerque departed for Ormuz where he arrived on the 6th day of the month of August. . . ." (Albuquerque, Parte IV Capitulo XXV)

With labor and delays Pero de Albuquerque received ten thousand xarafins in tribute from the king of Ormuz, with excuses of poverty in consideration of the tribute that remained outstanding, and threatening war, but not wishing to delay, Albuquerque accepted the ten thousand xarafins, ill content, and dispatched Tristão de Ga and João Teixeira to the king of Ormuz as his emissaries, declaring Afonso de Albuquerque understood how Xeque Ismael greatly desired to secure possession of the Kingdom of Ormuz, and that since Ormuz pertained to the crown of Portugal, the king of Ormuz was strictly advised—in no uncertain terms—not to permit any Persians of great state to enter his lands (*não consentisse que gente grossa do xeque Ismael entrasse em suas terras*). Furthermore the king was not to allow any Persian embassy accredited to an Indian prince to leave Ormuz with an entourage of more than fifty persons. And if Braz de Albuquerque, from whom we draw the principal part of our intelligence for the voyage of Pero de Albuquerque, has diligenced correctly, Pero de Albuquerque went so far as to ask the king of Ormuz to raise a hue and cry (*apregoar*) that no Persian, of whatever quality, should pass to India from Ormuz at the risk of forfeiture of life if captured by the Portuguese. This extraordinary intelligence is mitigated, however, as it is contradicted by Albuquerque, when in one and the same sentence he indicates the Persian merchants were welcomed in India. Moreover through his emissaries Tristão de Ga and João Teixeira, Pero de Albuquerque instructed the king of Ormuz with regard to sundry commercial matters, pertaining to the commerce of the horses that regularly came from Arabia and Persia to India, being matters of mutual interest, for the purpose of favoring the revenues of the port of Goa. Having gathered his merchandise, and ca. thirty-five thousand xarafins for the merchandise of the Moorish *naos*, captured in this voyage, and which he sold in Ormuz, and not having the fortress, or factory, Pero de Albuquerque sailed for India and arrived safely at Goa on September 28th 1514.

Albuquerque, Parte IV Capitulo XVI, Capitulo XXIV, Capitulo XXV & Capitulo XXVI
Barros, Decada II Livro X Capitulo I
Castanheda, Livro III Capitulo CXXVII & Capitolo CXXVIII
Correa, Tomo II, Lenda de Afonso de Albuquerque, Capitulo XLIV & Capitulo XLVI
Goes, Parte III Capitulo LXV

BIBLIOGRAPHY
PRINTED SOURCES

1. Albuquerque, Braz de. *Comentários do Grande Afonso de Albuquerque*, Imprensa da Universidade, Coimbra, 1923.

2. Barros, João de. *Da Asia*, Vol. 4, Lisbon, 1777.
3. Castanheda, Fernão Lopes de. *História do Descobrimento & Conquista da India pelos Portugueses*, Imprensa da Universidade, Coimbra, 1928.
4. Correa, Gaspar. *Lendas da India*, Lisbon, 1860.
5. Goes, Damião de. *Crónica do Felicissimo Rei D. Manuel*, Imprensa da Universidade, Coimbra, 1926.

PUBLISHED DOCUMENTS
1. *Cartas de Affonso de Albuquerque*, Tomo I, Lisbon, 1884.
   a) Carta de Affonso de Albuquerque ao rei—Cananor, November 27, 1514: p. 346, 347. Carta LXXXIX

DOCUMENTS
1. Instrument in public form whereby Pero de Albuquerque asked the King of Ormuz to pay the tribute owed to King D. Manuel, and the reply of the King of Ormuz—Ormuz, August 22, 1514. Corpo Cronológico: Parte II Maço 50 Documento 195 of the Torre do Tombo, Lisbon.

CHAPTER V

THE RECEPTION BY AFONSO DE ALBUQUERQUE, AT ORMUZ, OF THE PERSIAN AMBASSADOR WHO CAME IN COMPANY OF MIGUEL FERREIRA—1515

When Pero de Albuquerque returned to Goa from the mouth of the Red Sea, and from the Kingdom of Ormuz, he related to his uncle the particulars of his voyage, and told the governor of India that the king of Ormuz had accepted the headpiece and prayer of Xeque Ismael, and that the king was governed by a Persian named Rex Noredim (Rais Nur-ud-din)—who evinced a desire to deliver the kingdom to Shah Ismael—and that the captain of the king of Persia, who he had encountered near the island of Bahrain, dominated the Persian Gulf with a fleet. Afonso de Albuquerque, pleased by the return of his nephew, with the tribute and money that he carried from Ormuz, and fearful the Persians would seize the kingdom, and knowing the King Dom Manuel desired the possession of Ormuz, if it could be secured without endangering the Portuguese state in India, and desirous of the wealth of Ormuz for its own sake, in counsel with his captains the governor of India determined to sail to Ormuz and to erect the fortress which he had attempted in 1507.

Afonso de Albuquerque departed from Goa on February 21st 1515 with a great fleet of twenty odd sail, and crossing the Arabian Sea, arrived at Ormuz on March 26th 1515, carrying in his conserve fifteen hundred Portugals and six hundred Malabaris, all at the command of the great Afonso de Albuquerque, the conqueror of Goa, Malacca and now Ormuz, which submitted to the yoke of the conqueror without a struggle.

Having arrived at the Kingdom of Ormuz, Afonso de Albuquerque discovered that Miguel Ferreira, his ambassador at the court of Persia, had arrived at Ormuz. In his company Miguel Ferreira carried a Persian ambassador accredited to Afonso de Albuquerque, as we noted in Chapter III, with letters for King Manuel I of Portugal, and for the governor, and his present. The ambassador bears the name of Braim Benatee in *O Regimento que deu a Fernam Guomez de Lemos e a Gil Simoens que mandou ao Xeque Ismael* (which is only a copy), Bairim Bonari in Barros (Decada II Livro X Capitulo V), Barrim Bonat in Goes (Parte III Capitulo LXVII) and Coge Alijão in Castanheda (Livro III Capitolo CXXXVIII). Barros, Castanheda and Braz de Albuquerque aver the ambassador was the same messenger who in 1513 came to visit Afonso de Albuquerque in Malabar.

Having erected the Portuguese fortress of Ormuz, Afonso de Albuquerque desired to see the Persian ambassador, and greeted him in great state, having arranged to construct a dais at the entrance way to the fortress, with a high runway leading to it, carpeted, fashioned of wood and ascended by three steps, with awnings of silk cloth, a wall upon which tapestries were hung, and a canopy of brocade, beneath which were situated two chairs, worked in velvet and fringed in gold, one for Albuquerque and the other for the Persian ambassador, and to each side numerous cushions of brocade.

"All things having been prepared for the hour of the arrival of the Ambassador, Affonso de Albuquerque seated himself in his chair, dressed in the manner in which he would receive him, and around him the Captains and principals *Fidalgos* dressed for the occasion, and in order along the shore on [the] road by which the Ambassador would pass were placed about six hundred armed men, and other armed people of better quality (*mais limpa*) around the runway; and in addition to these armed people were many common people of the population of the City along the shore. At this time with his Governors and Mirs, who are the nobles of the Kingdom, the King of Ormuz placed himself at the windows of his palaces, where he could view the place upon which the Ambassador would enter, who was accompanied by D. Garcia de Noronha, as principal person, with many *Fidalgos* and *Cavalleiros*. The Ambassador brought the present before him in this order.

"Two men came on horseback and each one of them brought an *onça*-leopard which knew how to hunt and to return to his master, and these horses were presently followed by others caparisoned with sheets of mail, with arms to their use, and behind the horses came the present, which consisted of jewels of gold, pieces of brocade and silk, [and] uncut turquoise stones as they came from the mine, altogether [the presents, or perhaps the turquoise stones] would be worth up to three thousand cruzados. The said pieces were brought by men in *bacios*-bowls of silver *de agua ás mãos altos*, one before the other, and behind came the Ambassador with D. Garcia who accompanied him. And while he was feted with trumpets and kettledrums, which came in front of him, when he reached the shore, all the artillery saluted him with salvos, overwhelming the sound of all the other instruments and the conversation of the people, being as much as he had in the City.[*] The Ambassador ascended to the dais, to Affonso de Albuquerque on his estrade, and he raised himself from the chair and took a couple of steps. And having come to the Ambassador, each making his courtesy according to their usage, they seated themselves in the chairs, and after the Ambassador was seated, he placed two letters in the hand of Affonso de Albuquerque, one for the King D. Manuel, and the other for him; the letter of the King, Affonso de Albuquerque kept, and he gave his to the Secretary Pero de Alpoem, at his side. Having delivered these letters, the Ambassador presented the gift; and because among the presents came a *cinta*-sash of gold, and a sword, in order to please the Ambassador, by his request, Afonso de Albu-

---

* Braz de Albuquerque (Parte IV Capitulo XXXIV) and Gaspar Correa (Tomo II Capitulo XLIX) declare the artillery salvo was fired by the Portuguese fleet, and not by the guns of the fortress as Barros appears to indicate in this passage.

querque girded himself with both, as a sign of peace and friendship between them." (Barros, Decada II Livro X Capitulo IV)

Following the delivery of the present to Afonso de Albuquerque, the governor of India commenced to question the Persian ambassador for the health of Xeque Ismael, and for his wife and children; for the well-being of the ambassador and for his journey to Ormuz, and of sundry related matters. The governor dispatched the ambassador, bidding him to rest his person, and declared they would speak more particularly at a later day. Having dispatched his guest, Dom Garcia de Noronha, his nephew, escorted the Persian ambassador to his lodgings with the same pomp of circumstance that he had fetched him. Afonso de Albuquerque liberally arranged for the payment of all the expenses of the said ambassador and his entourage during their stay at Ormuz.

Two days later, Afonso de Albuquerque, relates his son, called the Persian ambassador. After the ambassador declared the friendship which Xeque Ismael, his lord, had for the Portuguese, thanking Albuquerque for the good treatment accorded to the Persian ambassadors who visited India, and offering the governor places in Persia for his use, if he desired them, he came to speak upon four principal matters. Firstly the Persian ambassador asked Afonso de Albuquerque to remit to Shah Ismael the duties of Ormuz levied against the merchandise of the merchants passing between Persia and Ormuz. Secondly the ambassador desired the governor to provide transportation for "certain people" wishing to pass between Persia and Arabia, in the region of Barem (Bahrain) and Catifa or Catife (El Katif). We have these things from Braz de Albuquerque and João de Barros, who are the principal sources of our intelligence for the reception of the Persian ambassador by Afonso de Albuquerque. Barros declares the ambassador was induced to say these things by Raez Hamed (Rais Hamid), a principal man of Ormuz, and by Abrahem Beque (Ibrahim Beg), a captain of Xeque Ismael "who came there with [the] title of buying certain horses of Arabia." Moreover the ambassador did not carry a directive with regard to the first two points in his instruction from the king. Braz de Albuquerque, to the contrary, declares the ambassador received instruction from the king.

"And besides these two things, he asked for a port in India, where his natives could find security for making their affairs; and thus aid by sea in order to take a place between the land of Jasque de Ormuz [Jask] and Diulcinde [Sind], called Guadel [Guardaré in Albuquerque, Parte IV Capitulo XXXIV, i.e. modern Gwadar], whence the Nautáques [people of Baluchistan], who inhabit that coast, depart with Armadas to assault the náos which pass that way, since that port of Guadel pertained to the dominion of the King of Macram [Makran], his vassal, who rebelled at times with the favor that he had from the sea. The reply to these matters, although it was not given on that day, was given by Affonso de Albuquerque at the time of his dispatch, saying that what pertained to the duties of the merchandise of Persia, which came to Ormuz, the expenses of the Armada continually em-

36

ployed against the Nautáques, were so great, and thus the expense necessary to sustain the people who went in guard and defense of the Towns and Places of the coast of Arabia [owing allegiance to the king of Ormuz], that in no manner could he deliver the duties, because the principal revenue of Ormuz—by which the state was sustained—were the duties from the entrance and departure of merchandise. So much as to the passage for the land of Arabia, and thus [a] port in India, and assistance to take the place called Guadel, he was very content [to be of service], provided the merchandise coming from India to Ormuz was not hindered through the port of Guadel and the *náos* were free to go their way. And with this reply he made general offerings to him, of little obligation, principally aid against the Sultan of Cairo and the Great Turk his enemies." (Barros, Decada II Livro X Capitulo IV)

Afonso de Albuquerque dispatched the Persian ambassador in company of Fernão Gomes de Lemos on May 5th 1515. Albuquerque died in December of 1515, and I am not aware that his promises were implemented by the succeeding governor of India, Lopo Soares de Albergaria (1515-1518), or by the governors who followed. Shah Ismael I died in 1524. Afonso de Albuquerque dispatched Fernão Gomes de Lemos, and fourteen Portugals with him, in order to secure the good will of the king of the Persians; for having seized the Kingdom of Ormuz, which the king of Persia deemed within his proper sphere of dominion, the governor of India was anxious to mitigate the ill-effects of a possible rupture with a timely visit to the court of the king of Iran by his emissary, who bore assurances of the love and affection that Afonso de Albuquerque nurtured in his breast towards the king and things of Persia. In his conserve Fernão Gomes de Lemos carried Gil Simões, his scrivener, and the author of the itinerary of his embassy from whom we draw the most salient particulars of the embassy which follows.

Albuquerque, Parte IV Capitulo XXVI, Capitulo XXX, Capitulo XXXIV & Capitulo XL

Barros, Decada II Livro X Capitulo II, Capitulo IV & Capitulo V

Castanheda, Livro III Capitolo CXXXVI, Capitolo CXXXVII & Capitolo CXXXVIII

Correa, Tomo II, Lenda de Afonso de Albuquerque, Capitulo XLVII & Capitulo XLIX

Goes, Parte III Capitulo LXVI & Capitulo LXVII

BIBLIOGRAPHY
PRINTED SOURCES

1. Albuquerque, Braz de. *Comentários do Grande Afonso de Albuquerque*, Imprensa da Universidade, Coimbra, 1923.

2. Barros, João de. *Da Asia*, Vol. 4, Lisbon, 1777.

3. Castanheda, Fernão Lopes de. *História do Descobrimento & Conquista da India pelos Portugueses*, Imprensa da Universidade, Coimbra, 1928.

4. Correa, Gaspar. *Lendas da India*, Lisbon, 1860.
5. Goes, Damião de. *Crónica do Felicissimo Rei D. Manuel*, Imprensa da Universidade, Coimbra, 1926.

PUBLISHED DOCUMENTS

1. *Cartas de Affonso de Albuquerque*, Tomo I, Lisbon, 1884.
    a) Carta de Affonso de Albuquerque ao rei—Cananor, November 27, 1514: p. 345-349. Carta LXXXIX
    b) O Regimento que [Affonso de Albuquerque] deu a Fernam Guomez de Lemos e a Gil Simoens que mandou ao Xeque Ismael: p. 389, 390. Carta CVII
2. Ramusio, Giovanni Battista. *Delle Navigationi et Viaggi*, Vol. I, Venice, 1550.
    a) Lettera di Andrea Corsali Fiorentino allo Illustrissimo Signor Duca Giuliano de Medici—Cochin, January 6, 1515 (Style of Florence).

CHAPTER VI

THE EMBASSY OF FERNAM GOMES DE LEMOS—1515-1516

The illustrious João de Barros, in his Decadas or *Da Asia,* excuses himself from noting the particulars of the embassy of Fernão Gomes de Lemos, after noting some matters pertaining to the composition and despatch of the embassy, and declares that Gil Simões, scrivener of the embassy, kept a day by day record of this embassy, intimating to his sixteenth century readers, by the purport of his narration, that a perusal of the leaves of Gil Simões must satisfy the reader's curiosity for a more particular narration of the things of Fernão Gomes de Lemos. The relation of Gil Simões never saw the light of modern day and the original has perished. However, three sixteenth century copies have come to my attention: two incomplete copies in the Biblioteca Nacional de Lisboa, and both wanting the name of the author, who is, as we judge by the intelligence of João de Barros (Decada II Livro X Capitulo V), the said Gil Simões, and from these two copies, printed respectively in Tomo I and II of the *Cartas de Affonso de Albuquerque,* and from a third and complete copy pertaining to the Biblioteca da Ajuda, Lisbon, likewise without indication of author, and unpublished, we are able to narrate the embassy of Fernão Gomes de Lemos in great detail, and to trace the route of his itinerary from Ormuz to Tabriz.

Afonso de Albuquerque dispatched Fernão Gomes de Lemos, and with him João de Sousa for second ambassador, Gil Simões for scrivener, Gaspar Pires for interpreter, Antonio Fernandez a musketeer, Francisco de Sousa, and nine other people, making in sum a total of fifteen, purposing to placate Shah Ismael for the Portuguese seizure of Ormuz, and moreover to respond by his emissary to the requests of the Persian ambassador received at Ormuz, and to have general intelligence of the Kingdom of Persia and of the Christians of those parts. Fernão Gomes de Lemos carried the governor's letter to Xeque Ismael and his *regimento,* which we print with our translation in Appendix II and III respectively, and departing from Ormuz on May 5th 1515, the Portuguese entourage passed to the port of Bandar (Bandar Abbas) three leagues from Ormuz, and in company of the Persian ambassador, where they arrived next day a Sunday. Bandar, situated on the *terra firme,* is a place of one hundred inhabitants with a mosque in the description of Gil Simões. To this port arrived Abraym Beça, the Abrahem Beque (Ibrahim Beg) of Barros, "captain of that land for Xeque Ismael," and giving credit to the intelligence of Gil Simões—our source for the embassy of Fernão Gomes de Lemos—we understand Abraym Beça had forty camels ready for the departure of Fernão Gomes into the interior of Persia, with purpose to carry their luggage and presents, and paying ca. one hundred and thirty-five and one-half xarafins of Ormuz, the camel masters (*almocreues*) were instructed to carry the luggage of the Portuguese embassy to a place called Diager *per* the Codice of the Colecção Vimieiro and Dragell *per* the Codice of Alcobaça, i.e. in the two codices of Gil Simões in the Biblioteca Nacional, and Diaguer *per* the Codice of Ajuda, being the "land of the said Abraym Beça." *

---

* In Castanheda (Livro III Capitolo CXLIII) and Barros (Decada II Livro X Capitulo V) this place is called Draguer, and in Goes (Parte IV Capitulo IX) Trager and Drager. These names are variants and Portuguese corruptions for a

"They [Fernão Gomes and company] departed from Bandar on May 11th in the afternoon, and they went four leagues all that night, and at sunrise they lodged along a very good and great *ribeira*-rivulet without settlement, [a] good land and way.

"The next day (*Ao outro dia*) they followed their way at times well, and at others poorly and without water. On May 15th they arrived at a *ribeiro*-rivulet which has its source a half a league from there; and the places by reason of the *sobidas*-ascents have water by pipes of wood. Here there was a house of a farmer who lived there with his wife and children, and he had great fields of wheat, millet and cumins.

"They departed on May 16th, and having gone three leagues from the place they departed, [at] two hours of the night, they encountered the foot-archers who went in search of Braym Beça, who were dispatched by Mizapiabudarra, brother of the wife of the King of Ormuz, [the] lord of Franguo Bonguo[*], because he had heard it said that certain people were joining together, brothers and relations of certain robbers that the said Braym Beça had ordered to be hanged, in order to kill him along the way. And from that place, and afterwards, they kept a sharp lookout, and they followed their way between narrow and jagged ranges of mountains with fear of robbers of the many in that place. And departing from the mountain ranges, they entered a great plain where there was a river with mills, and presently a league from there a village of fifty inhabitants with many fields of wheat, barley and millet, and gardens with many trees of fruit.

"They departed from that place and proceeded to another great place where the lord, called Myrjeladim [Mir Jalal-uddin], made great honor to them, and sheltered them, and gave them food and *mantimento*-provisions for two days. He is a well-disposed man of sixty years with three grown sons. The place is called Taurom [Tarom], besieged by [a] wall with its *cubelos*-cubes and *cava*-moat. Inside the wall are three hundred inhabitants and two hundred outside. The houses are of adobe, with mud walls, and flat-roofed (*as casas de*

---

place called Deh Gardu (from the Persian signifying "walnut village") as will appear in the narrative. If it is realized that in Old Portuguese the inversion of the first vowel and the second consonant is common, and the substitution of "l" for "r" likewise, i.e. if we invert the "r" and "a" of "ra" in the variants for instance, and substitute "r" for each "l" in Dragell, the reader will perceive the pronunciation is nearly the same in all instances. "Diager" is closest to the Persian "Deh Gardu".

* *senhor de franguo longuo* in the manuscript of Alcobaça, the *senhor delrey de franguo bonguo* in the manuscript of Vimieiro and the *senhor de frango bongo* in the manuscript of Ajuda.

taipa e adobes e terradas.) [The] water comes by conduits from afar. It is [a] pleasant place with much bread and many fruits, gardens, vineyards and dates, and many mills beneath the ground since the water does not have fall.

"They departed from Taurom on Saturday the 19th of May, [and] following their way, they arrived at Porcão [Furg] on Sunday, [a] place of Braym Beça, and they were lodged in a great orange grove of his, which had two places with houses and a great vineyard and dates and other [*] fruits and great rearing of horses and livestock. It has forty inhabitants, and around it many of his places greater than this. Here they were until Tuesday [May 22, 1515] whence they departed and arrived at another place of Braym Beça of three hundred inhabitants [probably Khair **], with many villages around it and people of foot and horse who came to receive them, with as many as two hundred of his horse and two thousand peons, over and above thirty-five of horse that he brought with him. From there they went to a place [Darabgird], likewise belonging to him, very near, of fifteen hundred inhabitants more or less, and it was formerly very great. He relates that it renders with its lands one hundred thousand cruzados, half for him, and the other [half] for Xeque Ismael. [The] land [is] very singular with great raising of livestock and orchards. Here they were for days because the ambassador fell ill.

"On the 5th of June they departed and went to sleep two leagues from there, and at another day (*ao outro dia*) they went eight leagues [probably to the Darkan of Mr. Le Strange], and the next day (*ao outro*) six leagues [probably the Timaristan of Le Strange], and they arrived at a great place called Paça [Fasa], with many seed-plots. And

* The manuscript of Vimieiro suddenly terminates the Portuguese stay at Porcão at this point, and resumes (in one and the same sentence) the account, greatly interrupted, of the Portuguese embassy as it nears Tabriz. Our translation of Gil Simões which follows is now taken from the manuscripts of Ajuda and Alcobaça.

** A book entitled *Mesopotamia and Persia under the Mongols in the Fourteenth Century* A.D., London, 1903, and another *The Lands of the Eastern Caliphate*, Cambridge, 1905, both by Guy Le Strange, have been of great assistance to me in tracing the itinerary of Fernão Gomes de Lemos. The Englishman has consulted the Medieval Persian and Arabic sources, and has delineated the routes which the merchants, travellers, pilgrims and armies *et al.*, were wont to traverse Medieval Persia. The Roman traveller, Pietro della Valle, who journeyed from Shiraz, whose barren hills I have seen, to the Persian Gulf by way of Fasa, Khair, Furg and Tarom (or rather a village near Tarom) in 1621, *Viaggi di Pietro della Valle*, Parte Seconda, Lettera 16, Rome, 1658, declares the route was little used, and surveys the stages.

41

following their way by these places they came to a *campo*-plain by a river of salt water where they found the wife of Braym Beça. The river was two leagues in width [Gil Simões appears to be referring to the Daryacheh-ye-Maharlu, which is a shallow lake rather than a river]. The wife of Braym Beça received them very well. Here they were some days in tents and a Christian died of fevers and the tents were sixty-two of the said Braym. In this *campo* Braym had guard of the horses of Xeque Ismael. They grazed at night and during the day gathered at the tents. At this place our ambassador dispatched the camels and took others."

The codice of Alcobaça ceases at this point, not to resume the narrative of the embassy of Fernão Gomes de Lemos again, and since the codice of Vimieiro terminates at the point annotated in the preceding quotation, we have only the codice of Ajuda (of those primary sources known to me) to give credence to Gil Simões. In due course we shall have recourse to the manuscript of Vimieiro when that copy recommences the narrative of Fernão Gomes de Lemos, after a great interruption, with the Portuguese drawing near the city of Tabriz. But not until then.

We left Fernão Gomes de Lemos and the Portuguese embassy in tents on a *campo* (or plain) close by a body of salt water two leagues across, which Gil Simões calls a river, but which we judge to be the Daryacheh-ye-Maharlu, a lake some twenty miles south of Shiraz. The codice of Ajuda notices the stay of Fernão Gomes at this *campo*, and declares the Portuguese ambassador and his conserve departed from this field on June 18th, and travelling through "singular lands," arrived at another *campo*, where they discovered a lord of three hundred tents, Bedijam Beça (Badinjan? Beg), a captain of Xeque Ismael, with his wife and house. Fernão Gomes and party were well received by Bedijam Beça and departed his *campo* on the following Friday, i.e. the Friday of June 22nd, accompanied by the said Bedijam Beça a league along the way, and Fernão Gomes de Lemos with company arrived at Carmaça (Qomishah), described in the codice of Ajuda as a place of one hundred inhabitants, with a very good fortress, and which in former times was a very rich and populous city, but by reason of rebellion had been largely destroyed by Xeque Ismael. At this town Abraym Beça (Ibrahim Beg), who accompanied the Portuguese from Bandar, received a message from the King of Persia bidding him not to pass ahead until further message. And when said message arrived at a later day, Shah Ismael ordered Abraym Beça to carry some horses which had gone to graze at Diager [Deh Gardu], a place ten leagues from Carmaça.*

---

* I want any notice from my Portuguese sources asseverating Fernão Gomes de Lemos passed through Shiraz, the principal city of the province of Fars, from whence we derive our name for Persia, indirectly through the Greeks. Guy Le Strange in *The Lands of the Eastern Caliphate* and *Mesopotamia and Persia under the Mongols in the Fourteenth Century A.D.* delineates the routes of travel from Ormuz to Isfahan, and proceeding from Fasa to Qomishah, the Medieval traveller of Persia ordinarily passed through Shiraz en route to Isfahan and the lands to the north. Hence I expect Fernão Gomes de Lemos

The Portuguese departed Carmaça (Qomishah) and journeyed to the city of Carma: in the codice of Ajuda a city of three thousand inhabitants, and a place enclosed by walls. By the phonetic appearance of the vocable "Carma" Gil Simões appears to suggest the city of Qom. However, from the tenor of his itinerary of Fernão Gomes, this is very unlikely, since Gil Simões indicates the Portuguese arrived at the city of Cayxam (Kashan) after that of Carma, and unless by some extraordinary circumstance (and detour) the Portuguese of Fernão Gomes de Lemos turned about face at Qom, to journey southward to Kashan, it is clearly impossible for the Portuguese to have visited Qom before Kashan. (Consult my map for the location of these cities.) I suggest Gil Simões intended to write the Portuguese equivalent of Isfahan, or in the alternative by Carma he intends the city of Isfahan. We have an important indication from Simões that this is so, since he declares the Portuguese, after departing Carma, came to an Alcorã (or great tower) fashioned from skulls of numerous wild animals that the Shah of Persia slew during a hunt, one winter, while in the neighborhood of that place. Antonio Tenreiro in his *Itinerario* (Capitulo IX), also gives notice of this tower of skulls, and declares it was situated two days north of Espayão (Isfahan). Of Antonio Tenreiro we shall speak with more detail when we come to relate the embassy rendered by Balthasar Pessoa in 1523-1524, with whom Antonio Tenreiro journeyed. It seems, then, by Carma we ought to understand Isfahan. But alas we lack assurance.

From this Alcorã the ambassadorial party passed to a city, situated close by this tower of skulls, and near a great *ribeira*-rivulet of many mills. The captain of this city, the codice of Ajuda continues, greeted the ambassador at his lodgings, who, when the Portuguese arrived, was without the city. The captain defrayed the expenses of the ambassadorial party during the time of their stay, and

----

followed precedent. Three routes were used between Shiraz and Isfahan. They are outlined on Map VI of *The Lands of the Eastern Caliphate*: a western route little used, a central route passing through the highlands, and described as the summer route, and an eastern road, today the main trunk road, passing by the ruins of Persepolis, via Deh Bid and Abadeh, and described as the winter road. Since Fernão Gomes de Lemos arrived at Kashan in July of 1515, as will appear, he undoubtedly journeyed by the summer road, by these stages, indicated by Guy Le Strange: Shiraz, Deh Gurg, Pul-i-Nou, to Mayin, Pul-i-Shahriyar, Rubat of Salah-ad-Din, Kushk-i-Zard, Deh Gerdu, Yazdikhwast, Rudkan, Qomishah, Mihyar, Isfahanak and Isfahan. The Spaniard Don Garcia de Silva y Figueroa (in 1618), *Comentarios de D. Garcia de Silva y Figueroa*, Madrid, 1903 & 1905, the Italian Pietro della Valle (in 1621), *Viaggi di Pietro della Valle*, Parte Seconda, Lettera 15, Rome, 1658 and a man of our blood and speech Thomas Herbert (in 1628), *A Relation of Some Yeares Travaile Begunne Anno 1626*, London, 1634, employed the summer route in their Persian journeys, and have left particulars of their itineraries and Persepolis. I am extremely provoked at the Portuguese for failure to note the ruins of Persepolis, especially as I am an ocular witness of their majesty, having climbed the mountain behind them on a very hot day in May of 1970, and surveyed the extent of the plain of Marvdasht, upon which the ruins rest, and upon which the Portuguese tread.

thus it was so in all the lands of Xeque Ismael. This place appears to be the Murchah Khurd of Guy Le Strange. I have seen it.

From this city of whatever name, the Portugals, pursuing their course to the Shah of Persia, arrived at the city of Cayxam (Kashan) on the Friday of July 20th 1515. Here the Portuguese found Mirabuçaca (Mir Abu Ishak), ambassador of Xeque Ismael who had gone to Goa when Afonso de Albuquerque gained it, and thus some ambassadors of the king of the Deccan (Mahmud, 1482-1518) and of the Çobayo (i.e. of the king of Bijapur, Ismael Adil Shah, 1510-1534), who in a body came to receive them half a league from the city with more than two hundred horse and forty musketeers bearing muskets of metal. The Portugals were carried to their lodgings and received "great presents". "This city of Caixam [Kashan] is great in trade and riches, and of great population by reason of the merchandise and foreigners who come to it. It is enclosed by walls with its *cubellos*-cubes and *cavas*-moats."

The Portuguese reposed for ten days at Cayxam and departed on July 30th for the encampment of Xeque Ismael or the Sufi, ten journeys from that city, in company with many people by instance of the danger from robbers, and passing by many cities and places, in the words of our manuscript, the Portugals arrived at the encampment of the king on August 23rd 1515, from which, the *governador* of the Sufi departed to receive them with many captains and up to twenty-five hundred horse.* The Portuguese alighted at his tents, which were settled in the middle of the *arraial* (or encampment), where they were until their cargoes arrived, which having arrived, the *governador* arranged to have the tents of the Portuguese erected near his. Having finished this matter, Xeque Ismael dispatched many trout to Fernão Gomes de Lemos that he had caught while fishing. From Ormuz, to this *arraial* of Xeque Ismael, the Portuguese journeyed two hundred and eighty-five "great leagues", informs the codice of Ajuda, and spent three months and so many days in coming "and the majority of the journeys were at night because of the great heat." The *arraial* of Xeque Ismael was settled in a valley besieged by very high mountain ranges covered with snow (seven or eight leagues from Maragheh, according to my understanding of Gil Simões, undoubtedly approached along the line of the Zanjan, from Kashan, via Qom, Saveh and Mianeh, after the manner of Balthasar Pessoa in 1523-1524), in which there were thirty-five thousand tents and more than one hundred thousand horses and thirty-five to forty thousand women, in addition to many other people, gathered on a wide and spacious *campo*.

From the codice of Ajuda we continue, noting that Xeque Ismael on the following Saturday (i.e. the Saturday of August 25th) departed camp for the

---

* This officer is the *vakil* of the Persian sources. In 1515 the office of *vikalat* was held by Mirza Shah Husayn Isfahani, appointed *vakil* by Shah Ismael in 1514 after the disastrous Battle of Chaldiran. He held the office until his murder in 1523. See R. M. Savory: "The Principal Offices of the Safawid State during the Reign of Isma'il I (907-30/1501-24)," *Bulletin of the School of Oriental and African Studies*, Vol. XXIII, London, 1960 and Jean Aubin: "Etudes Safavides. I. Šah Isma'il et les Notables de l'Iraq Persan," *Journal of the Economic and Social History of the Orient*, Vol. II, Leyden, 1959.

hunt, accompanied by eight thousand men of horse, and his governor (being the *vakil*), who alone proceeded in his immediate company, and the governor speaking with the king for a space, the king ordered him to return to camp, and to give a banquet for the Portuguese ambassador that day, which the governor duly hosted in his principal tent, with great pomp and circumstance, inviting Fernão Gomes de Lemos and all the Portuguese, and moreover an ambassador of the king of Georgia, and another of the king of Lores.* The banquet endured from morning until evening. The governor bestowed his principal notice upon Fernão Gomes de Lemos, the recipient of his honors, favors and bounty, who, with the Portuguese, Georgians and others, was feted with many viands and wines, consumed to the play of harps, lutes and flutes.

The ambassador of the king of the Georgians, and all his people, appear to have made a great impression upon the Portugals with whom they feasted that day, and the manuscript of Ajuda describes the Georgians, who attended this *convite*, as men of great stature and members, very robust, and very white, albeit men poorly dressed to the eye of fashion, but suitably arrayed for their clime in quilted garments of great thickness, by reason of the coldness of their country, and with hats of some manner of fashion or fabric—described in the manuscript of Ajuda in a manner that my ken does not comprehend by reason of the obscurity of the script. The Georgians were shod to the Portuguese manner.

At this juncture the manuscript or codice of Vimieiro recommences to speak along with that of Ajuda. And thus Gil Simões declares the Portugals, leaving the tent at the term of the said banquet, saw Xeque Ismael return from a fishing expedition, and they made their reverence to him, after the Moslem manner, by placing their heads on the ground, which the king acknowledged with the dispatch of gifts. With the two versions of the text of Gil Simões before us we continue our relation of the embassy of Fernão Gomes de Lemos.

"On Wednesday [the 29th of August of 1515], the governor told the ambassador to make ready the present in order to carry it to Xeque Ismael, and thus it was done, and many captains and other people of horse came for our people at the tents, and arriving a shot of the musket from the Xeque, they unloaded the camels in front of the governor, who sent to remove the goods and all the other things so that Xeque Ismael could see all pass in front of himself. The pieces were carried in silver *baçios*-bowls, and he was greatly pleased to see them and the cuirasses.[†] The tents of Xeque Ismael were settled on a *campo* along a *ribeira* and close by those of the queen his wife, and from there to a good shot of stone, there were no tents. And the said present having passed [before

---

* Lorestan? or Lori in Georgia? Identification uncertain; this name may pertain to a tribe rather than a place.

† A list of the presents carried by Fernão Gomes de Lemos to Shah Ismael, and translated from a document of the hand of Afonso de Albuquerque, will be found in Appendix I.

the king], they arrived to the Xeque in company of the *veedor* [inspector of the revenues] and *porteyro moor* [chief doorkeeper], and the ambassador coming before him, he kissed his hand and foot, and afterwards came Gil Simões, scrivener of the embassy, and he kissed the floor thrice, and he was attired with arms that the Xeque was greatly pleased to see, and he disarmed himself in front of him, and after him went Francisco de Sousa and Gaspar Pires [the] interpreter. Xeque Ismael was seated in a very great and rich tent *antretalhada*-in cloth work of form and *broslada douro*-embroidered with gold, on a carpeted estrade a *couado* [about three quarters of a yard] in height, and his cushions on which he was seated, and in front of him a tank of water in which there were many trout, and to the sides many carpeted pavilions in brocade. At the right hand of the Xeque was the king of Golym [Gilan], [a] man of sixty years to whom the Xeque was wont to make great honor, and close by him the captain of the guard who is [a] brother of Chynsoltã [Chayan? Sultan], a governor of Xeque Ismael who is in the field against the Turk, and at the left hand Dormyscão [Durmish Khan Shamlu *] [and the] king of Lores [see note p. 45], and the ambassador of the king of Georgia and two other captains.

"The ambassador kissed the letter of Afonso de Albuquerque which he carried and gave it to the Xeque who ordered him and all his people to be seated at his right hand between the king of Golym and [the] captain of the guard. On this *campo* were thirty thousand people, and after they were seated the Xeque questioned the ambassador and all his people for their names, and all of his people there, could not pronounce the name of the ambassador, save the King, who ordered the governor not to call him other than Fernão Gomes de Lemos in the future. Then the Xeque questioned the ambassador for the pope, if he were alive, and he responded he did not know, since he had been many years in India, and as one died, presently they made another, in such a manner that there was always one. He questioned for the number of Christian kings found in these parts of Hispania. He responded seven, *a saber*, Portugal, Castile, France, England, Germany, Hungary [and] Russia. Moreover he questioned him for the age of the king our lord. He said thirty-

---

*The respective offices of Chayan Sultan and Durmish Khan Shamlu are noted by R. M. Savory in "The Principal Offices of the Safawid State during the Reign of Isma'il I (907-30/1501-24)," *Bulletin of the School of Oriental and African Studies*, Vol. XXIII, London, 1960. Chicoltão (sic) is the reading of the manuscript of Vimieiro and Chelçotã(?) and Chynsoltã the readings of the manuscript of Ajuda.

five years. And how many children he had. He said four male and two female. He questioned for the governor of India, if he were [a] king. He said he was the captain-major of the king our lord, and for his knightly behavior he was made duke. And thus he was questioning and knowing what he wished. Then they brought him some metal arms, and the cuirasses, and lances, and crossbows and muskets, and all appeared very well to him, and he ordered a captain of his to arm himself, and settling himself, he fell upon his back and could not raise himself. The pleasure the Xeque derived from this, it is not possible to describe, when thus he saw him lying there without being able to raise himself.

"This having transpired, they brought food to dine, first bringing food to all the people of the *campo*, without table-cloths, and after they had their food, they served the Xeque in this manner. Before placing tablecloths on the table, they handed him water in a *baçia*-wash basin and *agomjll*-pitcher of silver, and he cleaned himself with a napkin of blue silk worked in gold. Thereupon they placed a carpet before him, and some circular striped tablecloths of silk, and they put to him food in silver *bategas*-bowls on a table full of *iguoarias*-delicacies, and to it, no other person arrived save the carver who carved before him upon his knees, and he did not eat anything until those near him were served, that was on table-cloths to his mode with many *manjares*-dishes. The Xeque with each dish he consumed gave something to the ambassa-dor and his people. After the tables were raised they brought many *baçios*-bowls of painted wood in gold, full of comfits and almonds and sweetmeat and sugar-candy, and they placed everything in front of the king, who shared these things, and many other delights, with the many people close to him, and *arredomas*-jars of very good wine, in abundance for all the people, and from his person he sent to give a *arredoma* of wine of Xyraz [Shiraz], which is the best found in those parts, and he ordered his governor to give drink to them, who by force made them drink, and thus to the Portuguese (*e asy a elles*), because a captain went shouting and almost striking whoever did not drink, who by constraint were obliged to drink from full cups and without water, and each time they were given drink, they showed their cups to the Xeque, and if they were not very full he ordered more to be poured, and he drank from a cup of stone inlaid in gold, that carried half a *canada* [a Portuguese liquid measure equal to three English pints], and at other times from a porcelain one, and by his own hand he poured the wine, and showed his cup to our people each time he quaffed it, saying that by himself alone he could drink more than all of them. The am-bassador said to him that he would like his wine watered,

and the Xeque ordered the porcelain cup given to him so that
he could take a full cup, and he rested three times, and gave
the *redoma*-jar that he had before him to his people, laughing
with them. And everything that he [the king] had before
himself, he ordered to be given to the ambassador, and by
the king of Gujlā [Gilan] he dispatched a linen of crimson
which he wore at the neck, worked entirely in gold, and they
were with him from ten hours of the day until night, and he
sent to give them quilted shirts of silk, and cloaks of brocade
lined with satin, and after being dressed, they were with him
a piece. And at this time they brought to the Xeque an
arredoma of wine from Portugal which Colejam carried,
ambassador that Afonso de Albuquerque found in Goa, and
he ordered it to be given to the *porteiro moor*, so that he could
drink it, and in his presence he finished it, and he said laughing, that he did not know if it were water, butter or honey.
Then the Xeque declared that since the wine of Portugal was
so highly praised, he wished to send a pair of casks of the wine
of Xiraz [Shiraz] to the governor of India.

"The governor of [the] Xeque dressed himself in our
clothes and placed a *carapuça* of velvet on his head, which
the ambassador gave to him with an imprint of gold, with
a figure for which the Xeque questioned. The ambassador said
it was Santiago, and he beckoned to the governor what he
desired, and dressed, he took them by the hand and said to
the Xeque that he was [a] Frank, and that he wished to go
with them. All placed their heads on the floor and went to
their tents, and the governor to his. And the king took a very
singular *bedem*-Moorish cloak from Cojolejam which Afonso
de Albuquerque gave to him, of fine black cloth worked in
gold, and he ordered them to make some pants of it to our
usage, and he ordered Gil Simões, scrivener of the embassy,
to give him a doublet he wore, and presently he divested
himself of it.

"The *arraial*-encampment was situated between these
mountains for ten days, and the Xeque continually hunted
and fished and continually dispatched trout, drake and wild
ducks to the ambassador, and on a Friday [August 31st] he
ordered the *arraial* to be changed to a distance of four leagues,
and the governor informed him they should go to that place,
and throughout the entire length of these four leagues, they
found neither end or beginning to the people of the *arraial*,
because the ways and the mountains to the flanks were entirely full of them. They departed during the morning and
arrived at the other *campo* at two hours of the day, where
they settled their tents close to those of the governor by his
order. The next day (*Ao outro dia*) the ambassador informed
the governor, that besides the letter that he gave to the king,

he desired to say some things to him. The governor called him, and took him aside in his tents with the *alguazil*-bailiff [the *vazir* of the Persian sources] of the king, and a scrivener, and he said all, and all the scrivener wrote in order to despatch them (*os*) to the Xeque, who had gone to the hunt for a few days, and then the governor departed for the king, and departing they gave him notice to change the *arraial*, and since he was departing, he left the person who would make the change, and he dispatched thirty horse to proceed with the ambassador and he ordered them to place them between the women, because Xeque Ismael ordered it.

"At another day (*Ao outro dia*), [on a] Monday September 4th[*] they departed with the *arraial*, and throughout the entire way they were unable to defend themselves from the women of the numerous great lords and captains in their company, and there was not a thing which remained hidden from their view, although with the ambassador they were not so bold. [The] women are marvellously very white, with headpieces of *framēgas*, quilted shirts of silk upon shirts of taffeta, French cloaks of brocade, velvets, satins, damask, cloths of *graā*-scarlet-in-grain, and thus they arrived at three hours of the day to the *campo* where they settled the *arraial* near a city by [the] name of Maragoa [Maragheh], three leagues from the place they had departed. On Thursday [the] 7th of September the Xeque arrived from the hunt, and the ambassador sent to know from the governor if he would dispatch him, and when he wished to see him."

On Friday September 8th 1515 Fernão Gomes de Lemos proceeded to the house (*casa*), not tent, of the governor, where the ambassador by word of mouth, or from the hand of the governor, received the following reply, *a saber*:

Why, if the Portuguese were numbered among the friends of Persia, the governor (the *vakil* or Mirza Shah Husayn Isfahani) desired to know, had the Portuguese seized Ormuz, that pertained to the king, and rendered annually two thousand xarafins in tribute to the crown of Persia; that the words of the Portuguese did not correspond to their works. Notwithstanding the king of Persia was the friend of King Manuel and was pleased to have his friendship.

Moreover, the king was not obliged to dispatch ambassadors to Portugal, as the ambassador requested, since the way, whether by sea or by land, was very long, and the king was determined to combat the Turk this year, and the king of Portugal would be informed of the result.

Furthermore, terminating the war with the Turk, the king expected to "understand" in the war of Mecca, i.e. to combat the Sultan of Egypt.

---

* The first Monday of September 1515 fell on September 3rd. Thus the Portugals have started to lose track of time. From this point, until the end of the itinerary, the day of the week and the given dates of Gil Simões disagree by one seen against a perpetual calendar.

Moreover, since Afonso de Albuquerque had promised embarkation for the passage of his people to Arabia, across the Persian Gulf, the king intended to dispatch Braym Beça (Ibrahim Beg) and Bedim Jambeça (Badinjan? Beg) with twelve thousand men to capture Catifa (El Katif) and Barem (Bahrain), which were his, and had revolted, and in this manner the king desired to test the friendship of the Portuguese.

Furthermore, the king refused to halt the passage of his people to the lands of Deccan, where his subjects were wont to serve in the armies of the Çobaio as soldiers of fortune. Since the Çobaio (or the king of Bijapur) subscribed to the law of Mohammad, and wore the device of Shah Ismael, to obstruct the passage of his subjects, as the ambassador requested, appeared to want either the rectitude of justice or the merit of good will. However, since the Portuguese were his friends, the king of Persia would counsel the Çobaio to make peace with Afonso de Albuquerque.

Finally the king intimated his intention to write to his captains (in the Persian Gulf declares Goes), commanding them to obey the orders of the governor of India. The king terminated this rejoinder by announcing his will to write Afonso de Albuquerque very particularly, for those things which had not been answered in this reply to Fernão Gomes de Lemos.

This reply (or rejoinder) having been conveyed to the Portuguese ambassador, the governor wished to know why Fernão Gomes never departed for any of the royal encampments, or for the land outside, and that this fact saddened the king, who always asked about it, since it appeared that Fernão Gomes suffered from some discontentment. Fernão Gomes de Lemos assured the governor he suffered no dissatisfaction, but to the contrary, he and all his people were exceedingly happy, since the Portuguese had seen the grandeur of his state, so that the ambassador, and the Portugals of his conserve, possessed a sufficiency of things worthy to relate, and since the king desired the Portuguese to see the things of his realm, beyond the confines of the royal encampment, Fernão Gomes de Lemos expressed a desire to view the surrounding country in the days to follow, and on the morrow Fernão Gomes and some (or all of the) Portuguese rode on horses to see the city (i.e. the city of Maragheh), which in former times had been a greater city, but had fallen into some decay, as "three parts" of same were in ruins, declares Gil Simões, but contained two thousand inhabitants, notwithstanding, and had a "very great limit" with many fields and orchards, gardens, vineyards, streams (*ribeiras*) with mills, and a great rearing of livestock.

On Sunday (the 10th day of September according to the reckoning of Gil Simões, but actually Sunday September 9th) the king once again proceeded to the hunt, and with the Portuguese ambassador, and with all (or none) of the Portuguese retinue with His Majesty of Persia. We leave the description of this hunt, rendered in some detail, and with some eloquence (and much force) by Gil Simões, for the pages of our Descriptions in Part II of the present work.

On Monday September 11th the encampment (or *arraial* in the Portuguese) was again transferred by the ever moving king, this time "near a great place called Bynado [Bonab] with many gardens and orchards and of many fruits and orange trees and cedrats."

On Thursday September 14th the governor informed the ambassador that the king of Persia desired the Portuguese to journey to the city of Tauriz (Tabriz), to await the ambassador that the king desired to send to the governor of India. Shah Ismael dispatched Fernão Gomes de Lemos with a present of more than three hundred cruzados in money of the land and a *treçado*-broad sword suitably worked in gold. And to Gil Simões, scrivener and author, and to Gaspar Pires, interpreter, and to Francisco de Sousa, of unknown office (if any), King Ismael gave one hundred and fifty cruzados, to each one in currency of the land.

"At that day the ambassador went to the governor where he found Braym Beça [Ibrahim Beg], and they embraced as if they had not seen each other for a long time, and speaking with the governor on many things, Braym Beça pleaded to the ambassador, that for the life of the King, our lord, and for the captain-major, to tell him if he or his people were dissatisfied with any thing not done to his will, saying the friendships of Kings were in the ambassadors. And the ambassador responded to him that he had no cause for discontentment, only of Xeque Ismael, who did not wish to inform himself of the things of Portugal and grandeur of the King, our lord, and since he had come and seen part of some things, he knew well how to inform him; then he would go content. Braym Beça replied to him that it was true that the Xeque [or Sheikh] greatly regretted the capture of Ormuz, since he did not know what had passed upon this. And being informed by him, however, he put it out of mind, and he would dispatch to the captain-major his ambassador, a very honored person, and very acceptable to him, with a present of five very good horses, and a golden saddle, and well-worked garments and cloths of silk and brocade, and *alboquerques* and *pinhões*, and wines of Tabriz, and a horse for Dom Garcia de Noronha. And Braym Beça said to them that Xeque Ismael would dispatch him with people to Catifa [El Katif] and to Barem [Bahrain], which had revolted, in order to secure their obedience, for which he asked embarkation from the captain-major for the said people, to which the ambassador responded that the captain-major had already departed for India, and that without his permission the captain of Ormuz could not grant embarkation. The Xeque presently knew of this reply, and he declared that all were excuses, that he possessed other places and ports where he could have embarkation, and that the *terra firme* was his, and that without it Ormuz would be lost."

*   *   *   *   *

"Thence our people departed from the *arraial* of the Xeque for Tabriz, six journeys away. They passed through many places and villages and lands well populated and well supplied with livestock, vineyards and gardens and orchards. Half a league from the city the captain came with many people of horse to receive the ambassador, and having arrived at the city, they were lodged in some houses of the governor of the Xeque, all painted in gold and blue, and surrounded by things full of water and three man-made tanks and their baths, inside a great orchard, where from the captain they were very well served with supper. Here they were for twenty days provided with all necessary things at the cost of the Xeque. This city has great buildings and very magnificent houses and it is populous. Many Armenians live in it. Their masses are of this manner, *a saber*: the Host of the same character as ours, only not so small, raised twice and the chalice one time, which are of our fashion, and when they raise the Host, they turn toward the people as when we say *orate frates* [pray brothers]; at no other time do they turn about, except [at] this [time]. They eat it as we do; the vestments of the priests thus like ours with all their adornments; images of ivory attached to a picture of the passion. Ten leagues from this place is a city of two thousand houses of the Armenians, and they [the Armenians] were badly treated by the former Kings, and after Xeque Ismael reigned they were well treated and honored. They have Lent as we do. They confess and make penitence. They fast very well.

"There are sixteen thousand hearths in this city of Tabriz and it is two leagues in length and a league in width without walls. Formerly it was [a] city of two hundred and fifty thousand inhabitants, and there are still large ancient buildings in this place. The Xeque makes his permanent residence here since it is great and very well supplied with many things. They departed from this place for Ormuz by another way, out of the way (*dezviado*), passing by many towns and places, [a] very well cultivated land and with great rearing of livestock. They arrived at the city of Caixão [Kashan], where they were for fifteen days until the arrival of the message of Xeque Ismael, and from there they went to the city of Vargim [Vargan], and from there to the city of Xiraz [Shiraz] by [a] route through many towns and fortresses and villages and great inhabitations of many vineyards, orchards and gardens and rearing of livestock. From Caixão [Kashan], from where they departed, to this city of Xiráz, they were fifteen days en route, not because the way was long, being fifty leagues, but by reason of the great snows they encountered, because when they made journeys, they had to clear the way with hoes in front, and by no other manner could they go. At the entry of Xiraz the *alguazil*-bailiff came to receive the ambassador with up to seventy horse, and he carried him to some great houses where they provided him with all necessary things for his maintenance. [And] being at this city Sultan Quelir [Sultan Quiler in Goes, Parte IV Capitulo XI], [the] lord of it, arrived, who had been gone

52

for much time, and with great happiness and merriment all the people departed to receive him, thus men as women, and arriving he dispatched three loads of fruits and conserves of many manners to the ambassador. And two days later he gave him a banquet which lasted from the midday until midnight, and he gave them garments of their usage.[*] This city was formerly very great and of very great and sumptuous buildings, and all the natives affirm the city once contained three hundred thousand inhabitants; and now it has three thousand, and another five hundred residents; and they knew when it was destroyed, of a thousand houses there remained one. Here they were eleven days awaiting the ambassador of the Xeque who was sick.

"From this place they departed, and by their journeys they came to the city of Lara [Lar] which is also very great and rich, entirely enclosed by walls and towers made of masonry, and *cubellos*-fortified cubes, and [with] very well made and sumptuous houses. The King of it is Arabian and tributary to Xeque Ismael. All wear his device. It has great breeding of horses and livestock. They make *tanguas* [and] *laris* [species of ancient coins] in it which circulate throughout India. It lacks water save from cisterns. And from there they departed and went to the port where they disembarked and they embarked and arrived at Ormuz safely."

---

* The Sultan Quelir (or Quiler) *ought* to bear a relation to the governors of Shiraz, Khalil Sultan Zu'l-Qadar and Ali Beg Zu'l-Qadar, mentioned by the Persian historian Khvand Amir (1475?-1535?) as ruling Shiraz at this era, and the Sultan Quelir of Gil Simões (or Quiler of Goes) seems to be the Khalil Sultan Zu'l-Qadar of Khvand Amir. In his *Habib al-siyar* (Tehran ed. 1954, Vol. 4, p. 550-552) a description of the flight and disgrace of Khalil Sultan Zu'l-Qadar at the Battle of Chaldiran (August 23, 1514) is rendered. Shah Ismael appointed Blind Solayman (*kur solayman qurchi*) to execute the governor of Shiraz; who returned to Shiraz after the Battle of Chaldiran, by what route, at what date and in whose company I have not determined. If we employ our quote from Gil Simões, it is tempting to declare that Khalil Sultan returned to Shiraz ca. November 1515. At any event we have some justification for this averance, since Gil Simões declares Sultan Quelir returned to Shiraz after a lengthy absence. When Blind Solayman arrived at Shiraz he discovered Khalil Sultan Zu'l-Qadar at a gathering with the principals of the land, making merry, imbibing wine, and listening to songs and plays of the instrument. Blind Solayman took the life of Khalil Sultan, not at this gathering, where he feared revolt, but at a house, where, Khalil Sultan entering a private room (*nehankhana*), Blind Solayman showed him his death warrant. Blind Solayman thereupon cut off his head and left the house. Ismael appointed Ali Beg Zu'l-Qadar to the governorship of Shiraz in his stead. The *alguazil* of Shiraz, mentioned by Gil Simões above, is the *vazir* of the Persian sources. He appears to be the Mirza Nizam al-Mulk Ali known to Jean Aubin, "Etudes Safavides. I." p. 76, 77.

53

Albuquerque, Parte IV Capitulo XL
Barros, Decada II Livro X Capitulo V
Castanheda, Livro III Capitulo CXLIII, Capitolo CXLIIII, Capitolo CXLV,
Capitolo CXLVI & Capitolo CXLVII
Correa, Tomo II Capitulo LI—Lenda de Afonso de Albuquerque
Goes, Parte III Capitulo LXVII; Parte IV Capitulo IX, Capitolo X & Capitolo
XI
[Simões], *Cartas de Affonso de Albuquerque*, Tomo I, pgs. 391-394 (The Codice
of Alcobaça), *Cartas de Affonso de Albuquerque*, Tomo II, pgs. 233-250
(The Codice of Vimieiro) & The Codice of the Biblioteca da Ajuda with
the Classmark 50-V-21, folhas 137-155
Tenreiro, Capitulo IX

BIBLIOGRAPHY
PRINTED SOURCES
PORTUGUESE

1. Albuquerque, Braz de. *Comentários do Grande Afonso de Albuquerque*, Imprensa da Universidade, Coimbra, 1923.

2. Barros, João de. *Da Asia*, Vol. 4, Lisbon, 1777.

3. Castanheda, Fernão Lopes de. *História do Descobrimento & Conquista da India pelos Portugueses*, Imprensa da Universidade, Coimbra, 1928.

4. Correa, Gaspar. *Lendas da India*, Lisbon, 1860.

5. Goes, Damião de. *Crónica do Felicissimo Rei D. Manuel*, Imprensa da Universidade, Coimbra, 1926.

6. [Simões, Gil]. *Do caminho que fizeram e ho que fizeram os embaixadores que foram ao Xeque Ismael e o presente que lhe leuaram* (The Codice of Alcobaça): Published in the *Cartas de Affonso de Albuquerque*, Tomo I, Lisbon, 1884. *Do caminho que fizeram e do que passaram os embaixadores que foram ao Xeque Ismael, e o presente que leuaram, e da reposta que trouxeram* (The Codice of Vimieiro): Published in the *Cartas de Affonso de Albuquerque*, Tomo II, Lisbon, 1898.

7. Tenreiro, Antonio. *Itinerario de Antonio Tenrreyro*, Coimbra, 1565.

PERSIAN

1. Hasan-i-Rumlu. *A Chronicle of the Early Safawis, being the Ahsanu't-Tawarikh*, Gaekwad's Oriental Series, Vols. I & II, Baroda, 1931 & 1934. English translation by C. N. Seddon.

2. Khvand Amir. *Habib al-siyar*, Vol. 4, Tehran, 1333 shamsi (1954).

PUBLISHED DOCUMENTS

1. *Cartas de Affonso de Albuquerque*, Tomo I, Lisbon, 1884.
    a) Carta de Afonso de Albuquerque, capitão e guouernador da India ao Xeque Ismael, Rei das carapuças Roxas [1515]: p. 387-389. Carta CVII
    b) O Regimento que deu a Fernam Guomez de Lemos e a Gil Simoens que mandou ao Xeque Ismael [1515]: p. 389, 390. Carta CVII

2. *Cartas de Affonso de Albuquerque*, Tomo II, Lisbon, 1898.
   a) Instrumento de Affonso de Albuquerque para Manuel da Costa, feitor de Ormuz, dar a Gil Simões algumas cousas para Xeque Ismael—Ormuz, May 5, 1515: p. 149, 150.
   b) Carta do Xeque Ismael que escreveo a el-Rey Nosso Senhor [1515]: p. 251.
   c) Carta do Xeque Ismael a Affonso de Albuquerque, governador [1515]: p. 252.
3. *Cartas de Afonso de Albuquerque*, Tomo VI, Lisbon, 1915.
   a) Instrumento de Affonso de Albuquerque para Manuel da Costa, feitor de Ormuz, dar a Amtonio Fernandez espimgardeiro, que vai com Fernão Gomes de Lemos ao Xeque Ismael, dous myl reaes em nome del-rey pera se vestir—Ormuz, April 22, 1515: p. 273, 274.
4. *Cartas de Afonso de Albuquerque*, Tomo VII, Lisbon, 1935.
   a) Carta de Pero de Albuquerque para el-rey—Ormuz, August 5, 1516: p. 166, 167.

DOCUMENTS

1. Letter of Fernão Gomes de Lemos to the King D. Manuel—Cochin, January 4, 1517. Corpo Cronológico: Parte I Maço 21 Documento 4.

MANUSCRIPTS

1. Codice 50-V-21 of the Biblioteca da Ajuda, Lisbon.

Dated Cochin, 4th January 1517

"Lord—Because my desire has always been to die in things of augmentation of your royal estate, I accepted the embassy that Afonso de Albuquerque sent to Xeque Ismael [Sheikh Ismael], having before me the service I would make to Your Highness in this by taking this way, which was sufficiently arduous, as you will see in the book [of Gil Simões] that is being sent to you of the said embassy, since thus it was long and the land is unknown; and thus because of the taking of Ormuz of which Xeque Ismael was not very content. In order to make this voyage I left a *nao* of two hundred tons by the hope that the captain-major [Afonso de Albuquerque] gave me of being rewarded [for] my services. After my coming, I found him dead, and with determination of coming to give account to Your Highness of what had passed there, Lopo Soares had for your service that I remain here, where I will serve in this going [of Lopo Soares to the Red Sea], which pleasing Our Lord, will make and finish what Your Highness desires and what those in your service here desire."

Corpo Cronológico: Parte I
Maço 21 Documento 4
of the Torre do Tombo

CHAPTER VII

THE PEREGRINATION OF FERNAM MARTINS EVANGELHO TO LAR—1515

EXTRACT OF THE LETTER OF AFONSO DE ALBUQUERQUE TO THE KING D. MANUEL

Dated Ormuz, 22nd September 1515

"After coming to Ormuz, the King of Lara [Lar] sent to visit and see me [by his ambassador bearing a letter of great offering "of all that he had in his land," declares Braz de Albuquerque, Parte IV Capitulo XLI], and he sent me a horse. Lara [Lar] is three journeys from Ormuz, a great city of Persia and obedient to Xeque Ismael [Sheikh Ismael]. To that place I have dispatched Fernão Martins Evangelho with *betilhas*-fine muslin and other merchandise of Your Highness to sell and to employ in horses and in any other profitable merchandise." (*Cartas de Affonso de Albuquerque*, Tomo I, Carta CI 1515-Setembro 22 Letter of Afonso de Albuquerque to the King—Ormuz)

Beyond the notices of the two Albuquerques, particulars of the journey of Fernão Martins Evangelho are wanting in the Portuguese sources. Notwithstanding he returned safely from his commercial venture, and perhaps successfully, as Fernão Martins Evangelho is discovered in India in 1517, whence from Goa he passed to the port of Diu to sell and buy merchandise as factor of the king, at the behest of Fernão de Alcaçova, as we noted in our volume of the Portuguese embassies to Cambay and Bengal, Chapter I Section 17.

Returning to Lar: the history of the Medieval Kingdom of Lar is so little known that a French savant of Persian studies, as recently as 1955, declares that Laristan has not yet been the object of historical research. Administrative insecurity, not less than the silence of the known sources, informs Jean Aubin, have contributed to make Laristan a *terra incognita*: "Références pour Lar Médiévale," *Journal Asiatique*, Paris, 1955. In the king lists of this monograph Monsieur Aubin indicates one of two personages occupied, and supported the doubtful dignity of the throne of Lar, in 1515: 'Ala'u-'l-Mulk (in the French transcription), who commenced to rule in 1478, but his death is not given, and King (or Amir) Harun whose year of enthronement is not stated, and who appears to have died in 1521 (but possibly later). The reader who can support the obscurity of a difficult subject and the French medium, will gather from Jean Aubin particulars of the medieval princes of Lar, whose slumbers are hardly regretted, or disturbed, by the princes of our present vain age.

CHAPTER VIII

PORTUGUESE CONTACTS WITH BAHRAIN, BASRA AND OTHER PARTS OF THE PERSIAN GULF—1515

While Afonso de Albuquerque remained at Ormuz, from the months of March to November 1515, securing the yoke of Portugal to the neck of Ormuz, the governor of India had occasion to greet many ambassadors of the kings and princes of the littoral of the Persian Gulf, who understanding the Portuguese conquest of Ormuz, and realizing the new alignment of forces in those parts, sought to ingratiate their persons by a timely dispatch of their ambassadors to the fortress of Ormuz, assuring Afonso de Albuquerque of their good will and desire to serve the crown of Portugal. The reader will recall the visit of the king of Lar to the governor of India, by means of his ambassador, noted in the preceding chapter. Amongst the kings and lords who visited Afonso de Albuquerque at this time are the king of Bahrain, the king of Basra, situated at the head of the Persian Gulf, and Mirabuçaca (Mir Abu Ishak), the captain of Xeque Ismael, stationed at Rexeer (Rishahr) according to Afonso de Albuquerque. Fernão Lopes de Castanheda avers the visits of Mirabuçaca and the king of Bahrain were returned by the governor of India, who dispatched his messengers to them. Castanheda has not disclosed the names of these emissaries, nor imparted particulars of their mission. Silence is golden but sometimes inopportune.

Albuquerque, Parte IV Capitulo XLI
Castanheda, Livro III Capitolo CLIII

BIBLIOGRAPHY

Printed Sources

1. Albuquerque, Braz de. *Comentários do Grande Afonso de Albuquerque*, Imprensa da Universidade, Coimbra, 1923.
2. Castanheda, Fernão Lopes de. *História do Descobrimento & Conquista da India pelos Portugueses*, Imprensa da Universidade, Coimbra, 1928.

Published Documents

1. *Cartas de Affonso de Albuquerque*, Tomo I, Lisbon, 1884.
   a) Carta de Affonso de Albuquerque para el-rey—Ormuz, September 22, 1515: p. 373. Carta CI

CHAPTER IX

THE VOYAGES OF JOAM DE MEIRA TO BASRA AND THE MOUTH OF THE TIGRIS AND EUPHRATES RIVERS—1517 & 1521

In that distant age when Rome ruled the world, a son of Hispania, Marcus Ulpius Traianus, better known as Trajan, succeeded to the leadership of the Roman Empire, and sought to reverse the policy of the emperors, who had with some slight exceptions, heeded the advice of Augustus, and had not sought to enlarge the boundaries of the Republic. In the afternoon of his life, and that of the Hellenic world, Trajan campaigned in Armenia and Mesopotamia and in the winter of 115-116 A.D. descended the Tigris to the head of the Persian Gulf. Trajan was the first and last of the emperors to gaze upon the waters of the Persian Gulf. Fourteen hundred years later another captain of Hispania returned to the Euphrates River.

The meagre particulars of the first Portuguese voyage to Basra are known from the documents below. Thus in an unpublished book of the expenditures of the Portuguese factory of Ormuz, Número 805 of the collection of the Torre do Tombo called Fundo Antigo, João de Meira, captain of the *navio São Jorge*, with Antonio Gill as factor of the king's merchandise, departs the island of Ormuz for Baçora (Basra) between June 15th and 18th 1517, with cloth, pepper, ginger and other goods to purchase wheat for the fortress of Ormuz, commenced by Afonso de Albuquerque in 1507, and completed by the governor of India, the same Afonso de Albuquerque, in 1515. From this same book I see that João de Meira returned to Ormuz with a cargo of wheat in September, or early October, of 1517, being praised in the same book for having well attended the things pertaining to the king's service.

Andrea Corsali, a Florentine in the Portuguese service, speaks of this discovery of Basra, without particulars and without reference to João de Meira, in a letter to Lorenzo de Medici: *"Balsera porto & città nel sino di Persia, nouamente da nostri quest'anno* [of 1517] *scoperto appresso il fiume Eufrate, donde egli entra in mare*-Basra port & city in the Persian Gulf newly discovered by our people this year, near the river Euphrates, where it enters the sea."

Alvaro Pinheiro, in a letter directed to King Manuel, dated Cochin January 12th 1519, speaks of this discovery in the following passage: *baarẽ catjfaa baçoraa etc. que ha dentro no Ryo fratees omde Joham de meira foy descobrjr segundo elle disso mais laargamente dara a cõta a vossa alteza do que llaa vay porque ho vyo// hate emtão nõ era maao.* . . . translated as follows: Bahrain, El Katif, Basra, etc., which lies inside, in the river [Eu]phrates, where João de Meira went to discover, according as he will more widely give account of this to Your Highness, of what goes there, because he saw it. Until then it was not. . . . The lacunae of the Portuguese text belong to the badly mutilated original (Corpo Cronológico: Parte II Maço 81 Documento 161). This letter of Alvaro Pinheiro is published in the *Cartas de Afonso de Albuquerque*, Tomo VII, Lisbon, 1935. The copyist, however, by oversight, neglected to insert the double bar // appearing in the original, which indicates the punctuation, in this instance period. The inclusion of the double bar //, in its proper place, greatly clarifies the meaning of this passage, as the reader of Portuguese will verify, and the reader of English may test by reading the above translation without the period. Finally, the same João de Meira bears witness to his discovery in a letter directed to King Manuel, who was already dead, unknown to his subjects in India, stating his discovery, but not very particularly, and describing a second voyage at length. Neither the first or second voyage of João de Meira are noted by the sixteenth century Portugals, in their histories, nor by the modern Portuguese, in their monographs, lectures and studies. Speak João de Meira! You are worthy to be heard. You are worthy to be known.

LETTER OF JOAM DE MEIRA TO THE KING D. MANUEL

Dated Cochin, 21st January 1522

"Lord—I do not believe I have written this to Your Highness in a letter which the captain-major, Dom Duarte [de Menezes, governor of India, 1521-1524], said I should give to him to go with his letters, the which is of seven folios, written word in word and carries six seals, three on one end and three on the other, in which I give minute account to Your Highness of all that you have ordered of me concerning the letters which Your Highness sent to the King of Bacora [Basra], and concerning the one thousand and two hundred *leques* which he promised Diogo Lopes de Sequeira, your captain-major for Bayrem and Quatyfa [Bahrain and El Katif], remaining vassal of Your Highness, and thus many other things of your service.[*]

"Lord—I say Baçora [Basra] has become [a] very great thing from the time that I discovered it [in 1517]. To this end and reason, lord, we will have trade with it, because now all the world responds to it. Here people fetch spices and thus indigo and clothing of Cambay.

"I, lord, went to Bacora on the 15th of the month of August of 1521, and I found so much pepper in this place in the hands of the Moors, that the *baar* was worth forty-eight *pardaos*, which they have purchased from that time that Your Highness gave quintals to Ormuz. The strait is very full of it. Hence it was very cheap. And many days were not wanting until a caravan came from [the] land of Xama [Syria] consisting of seven hundred camels, and they did not carry another thing save gold in bars, coined money, a great number of fine *contas*-beads, many velvets and veils, an infinite quantity of camlet, and saffron, and *papele*[?] *de mao*-writing paper[?] and many other goods which I have already seen in Portugal and an infinite quantity of mercury. Lord the pepper at once jumped to seventy, and following this caravan, much time was not wanting until another came of five hundred camels. I asked the King if such a great caravan was wont to come there each year. He told me this was not the case[?];

---

* This letter is lost.

that this caravan was bound for Aden and from Aden for Cambay, because each year it made its way for Aden and then Aden [Cambay?, the Portuguese is very obscure; in either case the proposition is absurd]. I wrote to him that it would not go [that way], because we were at war with Cambay, and they could not pass to that place. Thus for this reason, lord, he made them go before that other strait [what other strait?], which [is] not that of Aden.[*]

"It is sixteen days journey from Sama [Syria] to Bacora [Basra], and thus, lord, the merchants told me that for this reason they came to that strait, and since, lord, they did not find as much in spices as they had need, many of them came to Ormuz to sell their merchandise and to buy pepper to return, and it was their ill fortune to have all their *fazendas-* goods in the custom house at the time of that treason.[†] It appears to me lord that they will lose all. Lord I leave this. I say according to my understanding of this India, Your Highness has more need of one man only than of men. Your Highness assist it the earliest you can. One man before many men, because I have very great fear that all goes like [a] festival according to my perception, and wish to God I lied. I will kiss the hands of Your Highness. Commend to me a decree in order to go and licence for ten slaves who serve me. Our Lord augment the days of [the] life and estate of Your Highness."

Corpo Cronológico: Parte I Maço 27
Documento 97

---

* The king of Basra, to which João de Meira refers, appears to be the Ale Mogemez (Ali Mughamis in modern transliteration) of João de Barros (Decada IV Livro III Capitulo XIII & Capitulo XIV). I have found no reference to him in any Moslem source, such as I have consulted in translation, nor in any reference to a circumstantial history of sixteenth century Basra written in a Western language.

† João de Meira refers to the great revolt of Ormuz 1521-1522. Though in a smaller theater, the revolt of 1521 bears resemblance to the Sepoy Revolt of 1857. In both the want of prudence fed the machinations of Asia, which were conquered by the intrepidity of Europe. João de Meira was dispatched to India by the captain of the fortress of Ormuz, Dom Garcia Coutinho, to seek succor.

BIBLIOGRAPHY

PUBLISHED DOCUMENTS

1. *Cartas de Afonso de Albuquerque*, Tomo VII, Lisbon, 1935.
   a) Carta de Alvaro Pinheiro para el-rey—Cochin, January 12, 1519: p. 197, 200.

2. Ghillany, F. W. *Geschichte des Seefahrers Ritter Martin Behaim*, Nuremberg, 1853.

a) Brief des Jörg Pock aus Ostindien an Michael Behaim—Cochin, January 1, 1522: p. 121. I doubt, however, if the author of this letter, Jörg Pock, intends Basra when he declares: *Weytter so hat diser capitann morr heyst digo lopis desiguera hat das vergangen jarr* [of 1521] *gewonnen ein fast schonn landt in persia bei armus.* In any event his intelligence with regard to a *landt in persia bei armus* is minimal. The reference is probably to Bahrain.

3. Ramusio, Giovanni Battista. *Delle Navigationi et Viaggi*, Vol. I, Venice, 1550.

   a) Lettera di Andrea Corsali Fiorentino allo Illustrissimo Principe & Signor il Signor Duca Lorenzo de Medici, della nauigatione del mar Rosso & sino persico—Cochin, September 18, 1517.

DOCUMENTS

1. Book of the Expenditures of the Portuguese factory of Ormuz, July 17, 1516 to April 26, 1518. Fundo Antigo: Número 805.

2. Letter of Alvaro Pinheiro to the King D. Manuel—Cochin, January 12, 1519. Corpo Cronológico: Parte II Maço 81 Documento 161.

3. Letter of João de Meira to the King D. Manuel—Cochin, January 21, 1522. Corpo Cronológico: Parte I Maço 27 Documento 97.

CHAPTER X

THE EMBASSY OF BALTHASAR PESSOA—1523-1524

The ancient Portuguese were accustomed to endure the outrages of fortune with resignation and the provocations of man with the gnashing of teeth. The intrepidity of the Portugals overthrew the objects of their displeasure. Their resolution, a shield upon which a thousand bolts fell, and broke, animated their breasts and strengthened their choice. Their indomitable courage insulted the animadversion of man and nature. But the minds of heroes are often perverted by the vices of villains. Greed, not uncommonly, led the Portuguese astray.

After Afonso de Albuquerque conquered the Kingdom of Ormuz in 1515, the king of Portugal, Dom Manuel I, not content with the tribute received from the king of Ormuz, sought to extract from his client a more effusive sum. In 1521, acting upon instructions from King Manuel, Diogo Lopes de Sequeira, the governor of India (1518-1521), placed officials in the custom house of Ormuz, an act (and provocation) causing great offense in a nation of merchants. From the fall of 1521 until the summer of 1522 the Portuguese authorities were constrained to suppress a revolt in Ormuz. Valor, the child of war, commanded a conflict that prudence, the mother of virtue, might have avoided.

> "Before the Kingdom of Ormuz was gained by the King
> D. Manuel, who God has, the Kings of Ormuz paid tribute
> to Xeque Ismael, or Sufi, as they call him now. Afterwards
> they ceased paying it to him. And the King D. Manuel wish-
> ing to know the revenue of the *alfandega*-custom house of
> Ormuz, placed Portuguese officials in it during the time that
> Diogo Lopes de Sequeira governed India. For this reason the
> King of Ormuz presently revolted against the Portuguese,
> offering tribute to the Sufi which he formerly had from the
> Kingdom of Ormuz, with so many others, and that he should
> help him against the Portuguese. The Sufi was content with
> this and dispatched people in his aid. But when they arrived
> the King of Ormuz was already dead, and another King had
> been made, who was in harmony with the Portuguese. The
> captains of the Sufi who went in aid of the King, seeing their
> going was in vain, blocked the caravans that went to Ormuz.
> For this reason the King of Ormuz lost his revenues, and ex-
> cused himself to the governor, D. Duarte de Menezes [1521-
> 1524], who then governed India, that he could not pay the
> tribute to the King of Portugal that he was obliged to pay.
> In order to free Ormuz from this oppression, and from the
> people of the Sufi, the governor dispatched an embassy by a
> man of great merit called Balthasar Pessoa." (Tenreiro,
> Capitulo I)

The particulars of the embassy of Balthasar Pessoa to the court of Persia are gathered from a little known book of Antonio Tenreiro, a participant in the event, published at Coimbra in 1560 (*editio princeps*), and again in 1565. Of the life of Antonio Tenreiro, very little is known, save that he was born in the city of Coimbra, along whose streets I have passed, and who lived, married and presumably died in the same city. The dates of his birth and death are unknown. His book is his monument.

The embassy of Balthasar Pessoa departed the island of Ormuz, to the sound of many trumpets September 1st 1523, at ten hours of the morning in a royal galley (*galé Real*), which conveyed the Portuguese ambassador and conserve to Bandel (Bandar Abbas) on the *terra firme*. Balthasar Pessoa was accompanied by João de Gouvea, for second ambassador, Vicente Correa, as scrivener of the embassy, Antonio de Noronha, a Jew turned Christian in Ormuz, for interpreter, Francisco Callado as chaplain (*capellão*), Gaspar Milheiro, Antonio Tenreiro, a Moor called Abidalcalifa (Abd-al-khalifa), and thirteen other Portuguese who were servants, and whose names Antonio Tenreiro has not chosen to divulge. "Seeing the ambassador prepare for his departure, I determined to go in his company, in order thus to accomplish my desires, which were to see [the] world, and also it appeared necessary for me to change lands since I feared a man with whom I had some fights, richer than what it suits, for the quietness of whom I had fear." (Tenreiro, Capitulo II) Antonio Tenreiro was attached to the embassy of Balthasar Pessoa in an unofficial capacity.

The Portuguese were detained "some days" at the port of Bandel, taking horses (*caualgaduras*) to ride upon, and camels for their possessions (*fato*), and sundry other things for their journey. Our author, in a brief note, describes Bandel (Bandar Abbas) as a place of thatched houses, inhabited by poor people, living in a land well provided with dates.

Departing Bandel, the Portuguese travelled by land along the seacoast for five or six leagues through an uninhabited country to some wells of water where they discovered a few mean houses amongst a clump of palm trees. Here they terminated the first day's journey. Taking leave of this place, and proceeding upon their way for another three day's journey, the Portuguese of Balthasar Pessoa arrived at a place called Cabrestam (Kahuristan), enfeoffed of the Kingdom of Ormuz, and possessing wells of good water, some palm groves, and nearby, a great caravansary described as a large and vaulted one-story house of four gates, with a cistern in the vicinity. Cabrestam is a place heated by the fierce rays of the summer sun, so much so that Antonio Tenreiro, an ocular witness, declares he has seen men suffocate in the terrible heat of this land of Persia.

From Cabrestam the Portuguese left the Persian Gulf behind and directed their gaze toward the north and the interior of Iran. And travelling through a barren country, amidst some valleys of date palms and wells of good water, the Portuguese arrived at the city of Lara (Lar) in the realm and seigniory of the king of Persia.

Balthasar Pessoa, and company, lodged in the suburbs of the city of Lar, at that time a city of four thousand inhabitants, and were not very well received by the king of the land. Thus Antonio Tenreiro. According to Fernão Lopes de Castanheda, who died in Coimbra in 1559, one year before the publication of the *Itinerario de Antonio Tenreiro*, and who undoubtedly knew Antonio Tenreiro, Balthasar Pessoa neglected to make sufficient honor to the king of Lar, who was not the "true king" and insulted him by dispatching—through the intermediacy of a second person—a present of little value, which the king refused to accept.

64

Balthasar Pessoa determined to carry the present to the king in person, and proceeding to the king, very well arrayed and with a guard of musketmen, and on horseback, the ambassador was assaulted by a body of Moors, in a narrow street near the houses of the king, and was struck on the head with a club of iron, and gravely injured, as were some of the Portuguese with him. His people were assaulted not only in the street, by this body of Moors, but from the windows of the nearby houses with stones, arrows and darts. Strangely by some oversight, or act of volition, Antonio Tenreiro has neglected to mention this incident, and malice of the king of Lar.

Antonio Tenreiro, regathering the threads of our narrative from that primary source of the embassy of Balthasar Pessoa, declares the Portuguese remained at Lar "some days," where, by reason of the change of weather (*mudança dos áres*), nearly all the Portugals fell sick and had to be bled. Their condition improving, Balthasar Pessoa purchased horses, and the ambassadorial party proceeded on their way.

"We departed from the city of Lara [Lar] with the face to the northwest, and we went three day's journey by [a] rugged and wind-swept land. During this entire three day journey I did not see anything worthy of note. In a valley alongside a *ribeyra*-small river we slept in a uninhabited land with great fear of lions so that we always were alert with the horses to the briddle, and the mules of the muleteers that we hired in Lara, which carried the *fato*-possessions, were placed in the middle with many fires around. And those people with much fear told us there were many lions in this place, and at night they killed the animals of the caravans which took camp there. But during all that night we did not see any wild animals by reason of the many fires and vigil that we kept. This *ribeyra* [the Ab-i-Fasa?] runs from East to West and discharges into the sea of the Persian Gulf.[*]

"The next day (*Ao outro dia*) we departed from this place by the same land of this dominion [of the king of Lar]. Having passed a mountain range, we found [a] land settled with villages and great places of husbandmen, and close by: fortresses, rock castles and cisterns of rain water. At these castles and fortresses the residents respond when they apprehend robbers who come to rob them; because they never come [in groups] of less than one hundred. These robbers are Turcomans, natives of the seigniory of the Sufi. They continually live in villages of tents. They have some round white tents of linen upon others of woollen felt. They live by the raising

---

* Jean Aubin, who has studied this portion of the text of Antonio Tenreiro "La Survie de Shilau et la Route du Khunj-o-Fal," *Iran: Journal of the British Institute of Persian Studies*, Vol. VII, London, 1969, opines the Portuguese embassy, departing Lar, encountered the Qara Aghach near Karzin, and that the *ribeira*, which Antonio Tenreiro declares flows from East to West, and discharges into the Persian Gulf, is in reality the Qara Aghach.

of livestock and horses. They are a white and ruddy complexioned people. They wear linen of quilted cotton and much cotton and some fitted garments reaching to the ankles. In winter they wear linings of lamb and rabbit skin. Their women are beautiful. They weave very fine carpets of silk and always live in villages of tents and each village consists of five [or] six hundred tents although some of them are less. They ride on good horses and mares, which they raise, and [the Turkish men are] well armed with bows and *terçados*-broad swords or scimitars and shields of steel. They do not use lances, save in great battles. In winter and summer they are always in the fields because when it snows in one part they move to another with a more temperate climate. In all the fields and lands of the dominions of the Sufi we saw these people. They have the law of the Sufi, which is called *Rafaui* [from the Arabic *rafizi* or heretic]; that is they give Ali more honor than Mohammed. They wear the red cap. They speak the Turkish language. They call themselves *cazelbaras* [Qizilbash], that is to say red heads in their language. And what I have seen of these people is that they do not keep [the] law of [the] Moors, nor [that] of Gentiles, nor any other.

"Having passed the territory of this lord of Lara, we journeyed with the face towards the northwest. We entered some wide *campos*-plains between two mountain ranges: *a saber*, one on the side of the south which goes along the sea and Persian Gulf, which is not very high, in which there are great woods of cypress trees; and the other is on the side of the north, and thence goes running for a great distance, and the *campo* lies between both of them. From one mountain range to the other it has a width of eight *frazangues* [from the Persian *farsang* or league], and six in parts. This *campo* is six day's journey in length. They call it Coscojarde, that is to say yellow dryness in their language, and we travelled on it the said five [six?] journeys, and we camped near the villages of tents where we found all things necessary for our needs. Along these *campos* there is much venison and game of all kinds. Thus there are lions and ounces (which they fear more than the lions), wolves and bears, which make great damage to these tent villages, so that they are always enclosed and the tents are joined together and in the middle they make a corral in which they enclosed the livestock at night, and on the outside they have mastiffs as sentinels with bells tied to their necks." * (Tenreiro, Capitulo IV)

---

* Antonio Tenreiro's description of the itinerary of Balthasar Pessoa, between Lar and Shiraz, is not very precisely stated, and thus not easily delineated, but judging from the remarks of Jean Aubin "La Survie de Shilau et la Route du Khunj-o-Fal," *Iran: Journal of the British Institute of Persian Studies*, Vol.

Having traversed these plains between both mountain ranges in orderly progression, Balthasar Pessoa, Antonio Tenreiro and the Portuguese of their company arrived at Xiras (Shiraz), being received without the city by the principals of the land, with fifty horse, who accompanied the Portuguese to their lodgings in the suburbs of the city. The ambassador again fell sick, and this time with all his company, and as Antonio Tenreiro asseverates, three or four people died of illness, and the rest were cured by the excellent physicians of the land. During their residence at Shiraz the Portuguese were lodged "some days" in some "large good houses" possessing a great orchard and garden containing all the fruit trees found in Hispania.

> "In this city the governor of it made a solemn *convite* in his manner to the ambassador, and since it is strange, I will relate it. Presently they commence to drink in the morning some things of appetite, and it lasts until midnight or until near daybreak, if what they give you does not drop you; when they are drunk they cease. At these *convites* they have beautiful bottles of silver and gold and many turquoises and rubies inchased on them in marvellous order. At the *convite* are found diverse musical instruments, male singers, and female singers, who play the harp, and all manner of well tuned and pleasant instruments. They also give gifts and rich pieces among each other and they have great ceremonies in this. When a guest enters the house of the host, he extends to him a *fota* of silk, or another rich cloth, and as soon as he enters the door, as far as the place where he sits, he passes over the said cloth or *fota* with much ceremony and respect. And thus as he proceeds, the page of the guest gathers it without touching his feet. And after they commence to be inflamed by the wine, they rise on their feet, and make great reverences to each other and each one drinks a great *taça*-cup of wine, carrying a good *çomicha* [measure], and then they sit down, and they recommence to drink by another smaller *taça*, and they [the cups] go round about. And as soon as they are nearly drunk, the host has ready the pieces that he will present, which are *cabayas*-Turkish tunics of silk and *brocadilhos* lined with marten, swords worked in gold and turquoises; and the

---

VII, London, 1969, the Portugals, having crossed the river called Qara Aghach, perhaps near Karzin as Monsieur Aubin indicates (but I think further north, near Dasht-i-Dal via the line of the Ab-i-Fasa) passed the mountain range called Kuh-i-Maimand on the left hand, and via Maimand and Zanjiran, cavalcaded to Shiraz. The Medieval traveller was wont to pass from Shiraz to Karzin by these stages: Shiraz, Shahrak, to Kavar, Girivah-i-Zanjiran, Rubat Jamkan (or Chamankan), Maimand, the beginning of the Simkan District, the end of the Simkan District, and thence Karzin; See Guy Le Strange, in *The Geographical Part of the Nuzhat-al-Qulub*, London and Leyden, 1915 & 1919 and *Mesopotamia and Persia under the Mongols in the Fourteenth Century A.D.*, London, 1903.

host undresses the guest there and gives him the garments which he has and girds him with the rich sword; and then one is supplied with great abundance of *iguarias*-dishes, and foods of many sorts, and there the *convite* is finished. And they are so vain, and they concern themselves so much in this business with honor, that they go to whosoever does it best. The governor who invited us was very surprised that the ambassador and Portuguese diluted their wine with water." (Tenreiro, Capitulo VI)

Without noting another thing of importance, concerning the stay of Balthasar Pessoa and the Portuguese at Xiras (Shiraz), save a description of the city, translated in Part II of our Descriptions, Antonio Tenreiro declares the Portuguese departed Shiraz with the face to the northwest, and proceeding always amongst mountains and mountain ranges, including a very high mountain range on the left called Coaestäder (*Kuh-i-Iskandar*) "which means in [the] Persian language, mountain range of Alexander," the Portuguese consumed more than twenty days in passage to Espayão (Isfahan), and in the estimation of our author, one hundred *frazangues* (i.e. one hundred leagues or approximately three hundred and fifty miles). Antonio Tenreiro declares the Portuguese saw nothing worthy of note, but supplements this want of intelligence by these particulars: after each day's journey the Portuguese lodged in "some great houses" called *carvançaras*, where, in some of these caravansaries, they found a Moor who had care of giving the Portuguese all things necessary, *a saber*, straw, barley, cheese, raisins, "a thing made of honey," almonds and some nuts "which here in Hispania we call *torão*." In some of the caravansaries the Portuguese were fed *gratis*, since these places, as our author relates, had funds given to them for this purpose, and the food given to the Portuguese consisted of bread with honey, which they ate upon arriving, and afterwards meat according to the quality of the person. The Portuguese had great fear of attack by robbers in many of the passes through which they passed en route to Isfahan, but since they were joined by a drove of muleteers en route, and because Balthasar Pessoa carried "ten or twelve" Portuguese musketmen, these robbers "never dared to attack us," and Balthasar Pessoa's Portuguese arrived safely at the city of Espayão (Isfahan), where they lodged in houses in the great square of the city, before passing northward to the city of Cayxão (Kashan).

"We were in this city some days resting from the work of the way, and then departed for the court of the Sufi, with the face to the north. In the first journey we found some large and very good houses and an old Moor who lived in them. And the houses and Moor were merely for the service of curing some four tame ounces instructed to hunt, which the Sufi greatly esteemed, and by his order they were cured. On the second day's journey, coming along some great *campos*, we found a *curucheo*-tower of good height, made entirely of heads and skulls of stags, thus as [a] wall; and from the Moor who went in our company, we knew that the Sufi had ordered its erection in the time that he had made a hunt in the said

68

land with all his *arrayal*, which greatly pleased him, and that was his exercise. The said hunt was made in this manner.

"When he found himself in *campos* close by some mountain range he commanded all his army to arrive in three orders, *a saber*, he and his *fidalgos* in front, and the people of war next and the women in the rear. And thus they would proceed to the said mountain range, to the part where the game could not ascend, because he did not undertake these hunts except near very steep mountains cut perpendicularly. And as he enclosed the game with people from one side of the mountain range and the other, he and his *fidalgos* entered within and slew all the wild animals that they could, first with bow and arrow and afterwards with the sword, and being fatigued, he sent the other people of war inside to finish killing the rest of the game, and if they found a lion or ounce, no one killed it except him, because he dismounted from his horse and mounted a mule, since they are less fearful of lions, and thus he slew it. And this siege is not terminated until all the game has been killed; and the butchery endures for three or four days. In that place, in order to engender memory, he ordered made and erected, from all the heads of the wild animals which they had killed, a *curicheo*-tower with kneaded earth, of which, along the way, we saw some." (Tenreiro, Capitulo IX)

Having arrived at Cayxão (Kashan), Balthasar Pessoa and the other Portuguese took lodgings "in the uninhabited suburbs" but "in very good houses" of great antiquity, possessing sepulchres and rich monuments of the former owners, of whom memory is lost. By reason of the comparative mildness of the climate, the Portuguese passed part of the winter at Cayxão awaiting spring.

With the arrival of warmer weather the Portuguese departed for Tabriz, to which Balthasar Pessoa, Antonio Tenreiro and the Portugals of their conserve passed in easy stages via Cum (Qom), Saba (Saveh), Sultunia (Sultaniyeh), Angão (Zanjan), Meonaa (Mianeh) and Turcumandil (Turkaman). From Cayxão (Kashan) to Saba (Saveh) the Portuguese embassy traversed a sandy flat land of little water. The ambassador and his conserve rested a day and a night at a beautiful caravansary, in or near Cum (Qom), described as a city of two thousand inhabitants. From Cum (Qom) the Portuguese passed to Saba (Saveh) in three journeys. At Angão (Zanjan) they resided for two days, and were royally received and dispatched by a lord called Casumbajandur (Qasim? Bayandur?). "He was very noble and liberal of condition. This lord gave us a *convite* ordered to their manner, and with the pomp which I have already mentioned behind. [Tenreiro refers to the party at Shiraz.] The next day (*Ao outro dia*) we departed. This lord accompanied us, carrying some falcons with him, which he released along the way to catch birds along a river (*Este senhor nos acompanhou, leuando consigo algũs falcões, que pollo caminho hia deytando a aues ao longo de hũa ribeyra*), and in this manner he went with us a good league, where he made the ambassador and Portuguese dismount and in the *campo* he gave another *convite* with provisions that he brought with him, and having finished, he

69

dispatched us with great courtesy, and returned to his house." (Tenreiro, Capitulo XIV)

Passing through mountainous country the Portuguese arrived at a small town called Turcumandil (Turkaman), crossing a river at this place, upon (or near) a decaying bridge, and with the face toward Tabriz, the Portugals entered a land plentifully supplied with farms, villages and inhabitants, described as a very cold land, covered with snow when the Portuguese passed through it, which caused them great labor, since the beasts of burden, which carried their luggage, were constantly falling, and with difficulty were kept on their feet, and in motion. Nearing Tabriz, the Portuguese passed through a narrow pass of stone (*pedra*) and rockpiles (*piçarra*) which the Moors informed Antonio Tenreiro had been cut by pick-axe. (This is the majestic Shipli Pass, situated twenty-five miles east of Tabriz, on the main trunk road from Mianeh to Tabriz.) And with the face still to the northwest, one day's journey sufficed to carry Balthasar Pessoa and his Portuguese to the "most notable, largest and richest city, which they call Tabriz, in all the kingdoms and dominions of the Sufi."

Antonio Tenreiro renders a detailed account of Tabriz, in a description that we translate, and consign to our Descriptions in Part II of this work, which the reader will peruse according to the active dictate of his (or perhaps her) interest and leisure. Tabriz, the term of the embassies of Miguel Ferreira and Fernão Gomes de Lemos, marked only a stage in the peregrination of Antonio Tenreiro, since Tabriz, the capital of Persia, wanted the presence of Shah Ismael when the Portuguese arrived. Here they lodged "in some rich houses with [a] great garden and orchard inside, as in Hispania, where we were some days resting from the work of the way; and the governor of this city always dispatched to us our needs in provisions, barley, and hay for the horses. And some days having passed, we departed for the court and *campo* of the Sufi." (Tenreiro, Capitulo XV)

The Portuguese of Balthasar Pessoa departed Tabriz and journeyed fifty *frazangues* (or leagues) eastward, arriving one journey from the *arrayal* of the king of Persia. In this journey (or rather journeys) the Portuguese discovered many Turcomans and Allas (perhaps one of the clans of the Turkish Afshars *), and in these parts, Antonio Tenreiro informs us, his countrymen at times were wont to camp in tents which they carried, and at other times in caravansaries. The Portuguese saw a land of fields and mountains, and a land with grass, but without trees, save where they were planted by the hand of man—poplars, ashes and willows—in orchards and some other places. Antonio Tenreiro understood the people of these parts lacked a better fuel than the dung of camels and horses to cook their food, and that the land possessed an oil (*oleo*) called *natafe* (i.e. naphtha), used by the people for many household medicines (*mezinhas*).

---

* Among the clans of Turcoman Afshars are the Inallu, Alplu and Usallu; See V. Minorsky, *Tadhkirat al-Muluk: A Manual of Safavid Administration (circa 1137/1725)*, London, 1943, p. 16 & 165. Another explanation of this term "Allas" occurs to me. In Turkish and Persian the word for summer camp is *yaila* or *yailak*, and "Allas" may merely be a Portuguese corruption for the Turko-Persian, rather than the name of a people. Still, when Antonio Tenreiro arrived in Azerbaijan, it was not summer. In Turkish *aláy* means troop, crowd, procession or regiment.

70

One day's journey from the *arrayal* of the king, Balthasar Pessoa received a message from the governors (*gouernadores*) of the king, requesting the embassy to encamp near a small river (*ribeyra*). Here the Portuguese resided for "ten or twelve days." Another message arrived and the Portuguese departed for the *arrayal* of the king of Persia, and having proceeded half a day's journey, they were joined by many *fidalgos de caualo* (i.e. nobles on horseback), and arriving at the encampment of Shah Ismael I of Persia, they erected their tents upon ground assigned to them. Having pitched their tents, and gathered inside, the Vaciil (*Vakil*, from the Persian-Arabic meaning viceregent or deputy *) dispatched a present of food, and instructed the Portuguese to rest.

> "We were in this *campo* some days without the ambassador
> speaking to the Sufi or to his governors, because of their occu-
> pation in ordering a great *convite* which the Sufi generally
> gives to all the great and lesser men of his kingdoms and
> seigniories, who were called there; hence three kings entered,
> *a saber*, the king of Gilā [Gilan], and the king of Xiruam
> [Shirvan], and the king of Mazandram [Mazandaran], and
> two ambassadors of the kingdom of the Gurgis [Georgians],
> who are Christians, and border on the last lands of the Sufi on
> the side of the north.[†] I saw these people and thus other

---

* For a description of this officer, and the office of the *vikalat*, in its Persian setting, See "The Principal Offices of the Safawid State during the Reign of Isma'il I (907-30/1501-24)," *Bulletin of the School of Oriental and African Studies*, Vol. XXIII, London, 1960, and "Some Notes on the Provincial Administration of the Early Safawid Empire," *Bulletin of the School of Oriental and African Studies*, Vol. XXVII, London, 1964, by R. M. Savory. Khwaja Jalal-ud-din Muhammed Tabrizi held the *vikalat* in 1523-1524.

† The history of the Medieval princes of Gilan and Mazandaran is delineated by H. L. Rabino di Borgomale in the *Journal Asiatique*: "Les Dynasties Locales du Gilan et du Daylam," 1949; "Les Dynasties Alaouides du Mazandéran," 1927; "Les Dynasties du Mazandaran," 1936 and "L'Histoire du Mazandaran," Paris, 1943-1945. The history of the Medieval kings of Shirvan is sketched by B. Dorn: "Beiträge zur Geschichte der Kaukasischen Länder und Völker, aus Morgenländischen Quellen. I. Versuch einer Geschichte der Schirwanschahe," *Mémoires de l'Académie Impériale des Sciences de Saint-Pétersbourg: Sciences Politiques, Histoire et Philologie*, VIᵐᵉ Série, Tome IV, St. Petersburg, 1840. H. L. Rabino di Borgomale carries me to Gilan and Mazandaran, and loses me among a cloud of dynasties and petty tyrants, and I cannot identify his kings with the king of Gilan and the king of Mazandaran known to Antonio Tenreiro. B. Dorn, more to my purpose, declares one Sheikh Ibrahim II ruled Shirvan between 1502 and 1524. Since one of Dorn's Moslem sources declares this king died on the 18th of *Redscheb* of A.H. 930, i.e. on May 22nd 1524, the exact same day that Shah Ismael died, as will appear ahead, this Sheikh Ibrahim appears to be the king of Shirvan known to Antonio Tenreiro. The history of his reign is sketched by Dorn at pgs. 590-596. Ibrahim II is described by Dorn as a good and just king (*regierte vortrefflich und gerecht*), albeit one in frequent revolt against his suzerain Shah Ismael I but on good terms with the

71

great Moorish lords who came in great state. They call this *convite,* in their language, *mouros* [from the Persian *nouruz*] which means first day of the year. [The Persians celebrate *nouruz* on the first day of Spring.] For this occasion the Sufi had many provisions and commodities and very fine wines and thus garments of silk and *brocadilho,* swords appareled in gold, and turquoises, rubies, caparisoned horses with saddles lined with silver, and in linings of ermine, marten and *grifas* with other sorts of great value. And these to distribute to each one of the lords according to his state and merit. Presently in the morning of that day very luxurious and great new tents were erected for the Sufi, among which there was one, where he was, of extreme largeness. It was as large as the chief *sala*-hall of a king of Hispania, round with a prop in the middle as great as the leg of a man about the thigh, painted in gold and azure, and with fine tints and oils. The tent was entirely arrayed in colored satins with many flourishes, and carpeted with luxurious carpets, and with many silk cushions. The raised walls of the tent, made the tent much greater, so that all the kings and great lords, seated in order, could fit in it, and the Sufi a little further ahead: and in front of the said tent an *alpendre*-portico of the same trappings, which occupies [a] great space of the *campo,* and serves as a *terreiro*-terrace of the tent of the Sufi, carpeted with luxurious carpets, on which they make service to him, and bring the *iguarias*-dishes [of food]. And from one part to the other of the said tent were numerous carpets upon which were extended *fotas de seda*-coverings of silk, and placed by them, many large bottles of silver full of wine and small silver *escudelas*-porringers for drinking. And in front of the Sufi, bottles of gold and silver with turquoises and rubies inchased upon them, in vessels of gold, for drinking. And in this manner he made the *convite.*

"He ordered the ambassador with some Portuguese (among whom I was included) to sit down in front of the *passos*-passages [or court?]; and all the time we were eating, he continually had his eyes fixed on the ambassador, and at times dispatched *igoarias*-dishes to him. The tables, which were on the sides of the *campo,* were in space, from one side to the other, two shots of [the] crossbow. The *igoarias* which they served were generally of mutton and cooked rice of many colors, *a saber,* black, white, yellow and other colors; tarts and [a] pancake of eggs with sugar on top, *pão de trigo*-wheat bread made in the manner of very thin cakes. They do

king of Persia after 1518. There are not probably five persons in Anglo-Saxon-dom, nor as many as one in Portugal, who have heard of Shirvan, an obscure and extinct Moslem state situated in Soviet Azerbaijan.

not have chickens since they make little account of them in this land and they are seldom used. They spent [the] greater part of the day at this *convite*, and all those kings and lords gave drink to the Sufi, each one in his turn; and a son which he had there, of sixteen years of age,[*] kept drinking, and drank also like his father to the sound of many musical instruments, *a saber*, harps, flutes, harpsichords and others which we do not use, all being very musical and harmonious, with well turned and sweet words. This day having finished thus, the next day (*e ao outro dia seguinte*) the garments and rewards, which he desired to make, were distributed by officials of the Sufi. And they brought for the ambassador a *cabaya*-Turkish tunic of *brocadilho*, and a cloak made after their manner; and for the Portuguese, who accompanied him, and were at the *convite*, *cabayas* of colored satin, for most of them.

"During this same day the Sufi gave orders to erect two very high and straight masts at some distance from his tents. And on the point of each one [they placed] a thin and stiff rod on which an apple of gold, as great as a middle-sized orange, was placed. Near the said mast he erected a very luxurious *seibão* [canopy†] of silk, which is like [an] *alpēdre*-portico; and he, and the said kings and lords were seated below, and with bow and arrow they shot at the apple, which few hit, and in this he passed a part of the day. And presently many very well dressed *fidalgos*, with plumes in their *toucas*-turbans, came on horseback, and to one side, they made a good track for horse[s], and one and one they came a running, and close by the said mast they shot at the apple, and some of the dexterous and skilful ones hit it and knocked it down. And whoever knocked it down presently dismounted from his horse, and took it, and made a great reverence to the Sufi, and they gave to him a *taça*-cup of wine; and then they lowered the rod by a small cord and placed another apple on it. Each one weighed thirty *cruzados*, and two chests were full of them in front of the Sufi, which they used this day in the manner thus stated.

* The reference is to Tahmasp—the next king of Persia. Barros (Decada III Livro VII Capitolo IX) and Castanheda (Livro VI Capitolo XLVII) aver the youth was fifteen at this time. However, Moslem history declares Tahmasp was ten years of age; Cf. Ghulam Sarwar, *History of Shah Isma'il Safawi*, Aligarh, 1939. Gil Simões appears to confirm Sarwar. Finally, if we admit Tahmasp was sufficiently bright to know his age at this time, and given by the king in his *Memoirs*, we are bound to hold the lad was ten years old; See Paul Horn, "Die Denkwürdigkeiten des Šah Tahmasp I von Persien," *Zeitschrift der Deutschen Morgenländischen Gesellschaft*, Band 44, Leipzig, 1890, at p. 576.
† From the Persian *sayaban*, meaning umbrella or parasol or canopy.

"The following day the Sufi ordered that they would carry the present to him which the Governor D. Duarte de Menezes and the King of Ormuz dispatched to him; being [from the king of Ormuz] many very fine pieces of *beatilha*-fine muslin from Bengal, jars of ginger conserve, a piece of amber as great as the head of a man, some rings of rich rubies and diamonds, a great twisted porcelain piece as large as a wheel of a cart. The present of D. Duarte consisted of well gilded silver-plate with *bastiães*: a *saber*, a chamberpot *dagoa as mãos*, pitcher and salt-box and two great *taças*-drinking cups; a saddle with stirrups, and [a] chest and [a] well gilded poitrel with filigree; two pieces or silk cushions, and the curtains and complement for a *leyto*-bed of silk made in the Portuguese manner, and a complete body of very well wrought arms. And placed in item, they were placed in his hand. Then he departed from the tent and sat upon a *leyto*-couch, that they furnished for him, to which the ambassador came, and by Moors all the present[s] were passed before him. They carried one in front of the other. And the Sufi inspected none of these pieces, nor made account of them, save the arms which I wore. And to show how much he was pleased to see them, he detained me, and spoke with me, and he took a gauntlet from me and placed it on his hand; and presently he called one, his confidant, and made him put on the armor, and said to him: 'Will you thus go with me this journey?' And presently he sent for the porcelain container and told them to fill it with wine because everyone was obliged to drink.

"[It was the] ancient custom of the kings of Persia, that so much more they could drink without becoming drunk, so much more were they esteemed. And thus they filled the porcelain container, and he took a good quantity of wine; and at times the Sufi drank of the wine from the porcelain container, but he was little affected by it. And in this interval, the lords who were around him, were jesting and making merry. After taking it he delivered it to the kings and lords around him, making ribald jokes as he proceeded, which I could well hear since I was near him. Having terminated this, he mounted a horse, and with [those] Moors and lords, his companions, he commenced to wander away from the way of the *arrayal*, and he carried falcons and dogs with him. And during the time that we were in this *arrayal*, many Persian Moors, male and female, came in *magotes*-crowds in most of those days: and they arrived at the *arrayal* with many sounds of instruments and with great merriment. And as they arrived, the Sufi was informed, and in full dress he departed from the tent with his sword at the waist in his *talabartes*-sword belt[s?]. And presently, in order to make much honor and welcome to these people, he drank a *taça*-cup of wine in front of them. And they beheaded a cow in front of him in the manner of [a] sacrifice: and they uttered a great shout, declaring no evil could now come to them in their lives. And those who had horses, or mares, or beautiful daughters, offered them to him: and this being done, they departed very well satisfied and content for their lands. And I saw this many times in the time that I was in this *arrayal*, in which they told us that at least thirty thousand people of horse were there, and moreover, twenty thousand tents; and three or four great lords were continually there with tents almost as large as those of the Sufi, and they brought with them trumpets, *anafiles*-Moorish trumpets and great and small kettledrums; which they strike for a good hour at sunrise. They also bring their wives with them in other tents, as large as theirs, which they erect behind theirs, and adjoining them.

"When he breaks camp, all the wives of the servants of the Sufi join, to one side, behind his wives. They are very well dressed, and [ride] on the best horses which their husbands have, and with [the] best accouterments, riding on them as the men do; and in their attire they do not dress differently than the men, save they wear some *garauins*-headdresses on the head with *trançados*-braids in back, and the face veiled. And in front, between them and the saddlebow, some little satin cushions, upon which they lean for *gentileza*. The men, in the same manner, are dressed with the best garments that they have, *a saber*, *cabayas* of silk, robes of velvet, and scarlet, and violet cloths; and those who lack silk, [dress] with very fine quilted white and blue linen, and lined blue cloaks of [or from] London, leggings upon draws of cloth, likewise blue, with complete *piar*, and very sturdy shoes of leather, and the soles fastened with numerous small iron nails, and at the heels an attached *escudete*-plate of iron, with a point of one *polegada*-inch, which serves as [a] spur. They gird themselves with some folded *talabartes*-sword belts of slender leather, worked in iron, in which they wear their sword with a sharp edge, four spans in length, and distinguished by its *cota*-coat of mail, and made of very fine steel, falling transeversely upon the thigh. They always keep the head and beard closely cut, save for the upper lip which they always leave unshaven; and this so long as they are young and without gray hair, and after they begin to have gray hair, they allow the beard to grow and wear it long. Their horses are large and strong, and their trappings are saddles with long stirrups with *loros*-stirrup straps and girth as a *gineta* [jennet]. The *estribos*-stirrups are like [the] *ariçaueis*-stirrups of [the] beasts of ancient times, however with more iron, and the bit is nearly *ginete*, and with less iron, with tight fitting headstalls, and cruppers, and [a] poitrel entirely quilted, and many of them painted in blue and in oils, like some of their saddles, and on the hips of the horses some coverings of silk or *brocadilho*, which covers all, with *forcadura de retros*-splitting of silk of colors. The majority of them bear bows and arrows in time of peace, and in war they add very strong skirts of mail, and half lances, with iron points like *zagunchos, de astes*-javelins, with staffs, painted in red, and green, and with little silken streamers of colors. When this *arrayal* settles in [a] flat land, which seldom happens, it occupies so much space of land, that many times I saw birds flying across it, and the Moors from all sides raising a shout, they fell among the tents, and they took them in hand. Half a league from this *arrayal*, at times more, there is continually another *arrayal* of pleasing tents, in which are found many merchants who bring all [kinds of] merchandise: *a saber*, garments made of silk in costly linings, caparisons for horses, and well made saddles; wheat, barley, and meats, butter, and fruits, and rice, and cooks who sell all [kinds of] food very well cooked. They call this *arrayal: Ordubuzar* [from the Persian *ordu*-camp + *bazar*], which means *arrayal* [or encampment] of [the] market place, where many Moors are continually, and it appears like a great fair. This *arrayal* provides for that of the Sufi." (Tenreiro, Capitulo XVII)

The Persians changed the *arrayal* or encampment to take advantage of new pasture grounds; the horses and camels with their appetites and heavy feet, making a change necessary. The Persians arrived close by some mountains enclosing the Caspian Sea from the west (probably the Reshteh-ye-Boghrov Dagh), where they remained for a few days, and the Portuguese of Balthasar Pessoa with them. Again camp was raised and the Persians removed to fields and mountains near the town of Ardiuil (Ardabil), a very populous and honored *villa*, in the words of Antonio Tenreiro, with fields abounding in wheat, barley and fruits as Hispania, formerly the city of Xequeaidar (Sheikh Haidar) father of Shah Ismael, buried in a notable mosque in this city.

In the vicinity of Ardiuil the Portuguese were informed of the illness, and approaching death of the Sufi. Fearing they would be robbed, if Shah Ismael died, and expecting, and attempting to secure themselves against the dangers of a disputed succession, they retreated to a secluded caravansary nearby, which they guarded with guns, and then to Tabriz by horses, with the greatest dispatch, covering all (or a great part) of the distance from the *arrayal* of the Sufi, to Tabriz, in three days and nights without rest, allowing the horses only some moments to eat. At Tabriz the Portugals were informed of the death of Shah Ismael which occurred on the 18th of Rajab A.H. 930 (May 22nd 1524), according to the Persian historian Hasan-i-Rumlu. He was succeeded by his son Tahmasp, a vigorous youth of ten (or sixteen) years. A state of anarchy reigned in Persia. Antonio Tenreiro records a great lord of the Sufi arrived at Tabriz, three or four days after the Portuguese, with many men of horse, and secured the city for the new king, and threatened the populace with vengeance, in the event of disturbances. During these days the Portugals kept watch with arms in hand, and with loaded guns, and well enclosed in the houses where they lodged in their first arrival at Tabriz.

This lord of the new Sufi continually patrolled Tabriz with his horsemen. The stalls of the merchants were reopened. News arrived that Shah Tahmasp had arrived three day's distance from Tabriz to the east. "And after arriving there with his *arrayal*, he took account of the treasurers of his father, and since they did not give good account, he sent to make cruel justice to some of them, and to others he took as much as they had; thus he also killed great lords who had faults with his own hand with blows of the sword. Finished making these cruelties to men, he ordered lions and bears fetched, and he killed them. And he did all this to engender fear of himself, because this is thus the custom of the Moorish lords of these lands." (Tenreiro, Capitulo XIX) Having passed "some days" (Tenreiro is always neglectful, never precise, about dates), the ambassador Balthasar Pessoa departed for the *arrayal* of the new shah to render his embassy, and Antonio Tenreiro separated from the conserve of his countrymen, and departed Tabriz for Jerusalem "which I greatly desired to see" in company of seven Armenian Christians, way of Armenia.

The itinerary of Antonio Tenreiro in Armenia, Syria and beyond does not concern our Persian narrative, which in this year of 1524, has exceeded by three years our customary term in those works already published of my *First Age of the Portuguese Embassies, Navigations and Peregrinations*. With the departure of Antonio Tenreiro from the conserve of Balthasar Pessoa, we, alas, want a narrative of the conclusion of the embassy. Fernão Lopes de Castanheda merely affirms the new king, Thamaz (Tahmasp), dispatched Balthasar Pessoa "without conceding anything he asked, nor making any instance of him, and thus he returned discontent [to Ormuz]." (Castanheda, Livro VI Capitolo XLVII)

Barros, Decada III Livro VII Capitulo IX
Castanheda, Livro VI Capitolo XLVI & Capitolo XLVII
Tenreiro, Capitulo I to Capitulo XX

BIBLIOGRAPHY
PRINTED SOURCES
PORTUGUESE

1. Barros, João de. *Da Asia*, Vol. 6, Lisbon, 1777.
2. Castanheda, Fernão Lopes de. *História do Descobrimento & Conquista da India pelos Portugueses*, Imprensa da Universidade, Coimbra, 1929.
3. Tenreiro, Antonio. *Itinerario de Antonio Tenrreyro*, Coimbra, 1565. Cf. *Itinerários da India a Portugal por Terra*, Imprensa da Universidade, Coimbra, 1923, edited by António Baião.

PERSIAN

1. Hasan-i-Rumlu. *A Chronicle of the Early Safawis, being the Ahsanu't-Tawarikh*, Gaekwad's Oriental Series, Vols. I & II, Baroda, 1931 & 1934. English translation by C. N. Seddon.

2. Shah Tahmasp. *Memoirs*. Persian text published by Paul Horn, "Die Denk-würdigkeiten des Šah Tahmasp I von Persien," *Zeitschrift der Deutschen Morgenländischen Gesellschaft*, Band 44, Leipzig, 1890.

Documents

1. Letter of Balthasar Pessoa to King D. João III. Fragmentos: Documentos da India, Cartas Missivas. This letter, which is badly damaged, pertains to an unorganized collection of the Torre do Tombo called the "Fragmentos" and wants any notice of author, date or place where written, other than a note which I wrote in Portuguese upon the folder protecting this document, to wit, that it was written by Balthasar Pessoa, shortly before his departure to the court of Xeque Ismael.

PART II

DESCRIPTIONS

CHAPTER XI

DESCRIPTION OF THE KINGDOM AND CITY OF LAR
BY ANTONIO TENREIRO

"The city of Lara [Lar] is in the dominion of Persia, situated between some mountain ranges, further west than Ormuz. It is enclosed by [a] very strong wall of stone and plaster, and in part it has throws of glazed tiles, which give a very good appearance. Inside are very good houses with French walls (*taypas francesas*). The roads are well laid out. There are four thousand inhabitants, all Moors of the white race, called Laris. They wear cloths of linen, with quilted cotton in winter, and in the summer they gird it about themselves, and *ceroulas*-draws, [and] shoes with points turned upwards. They are made of strips of cotton cloth, thus the pieces, as the soles, and they wear for a long time. They make very prime and strong Turkish bows in this city; and since this is so, they carry them for sundry parts, where they are greatly esteemed, and they say a bow of Lara, as we say a helmet of Milan. And they wear unwrapped turbans (*toucas foteadas*) on their heads and *fotas* of *seto*.[*] Some wear the *carapução*-cap of the Sufi [being Shah Ismael] beneath them.

"The principal *mantimento*-sustenance of the land are dates, and barley in great abundance, from which they make some *boleymas*-cakes. It is also provided with wheat but not so much. The meat which they eat is from [the] goat and from mountain animals, which they kill with bows [and arrows], at which they are very dexterous. And thus always in time of war, as of peace, they carry them with them.

"The King does not have great estate. Outside of it [i.e. outside of the city] near to the walls [are] *quintaãs*-villas of great and noble settlements of groves with fruit, as here in Hispania, and palm trees with dates. In this city live some Persian Jews, poor people, natives of the same land. The money which they call *Larim* is struck here. It is worth three *vintẽs*. There are many muleteers in this land. Each one has seven, or fourteen, or twenty-one mules, and they call each group of seven a *catar*, that is to say [a] drove; and they say a man is [a] muleteer of a *catar*, or two; and they journey throughout all of Persia, carrying merchandise very securely from some cities to others, who robbers dare not attack, since they are very forceful, and always go prepared with good

---

* *fotas*-turbans; *seto*-a kind of silk.

arms, *a saber*: bows, arrows and shields of steel and good scimitars. . . . [Here follows a digression of Tenreiro, neither factual or germane, upon Tamerlane. The author claims the people of Lar declare Tamerlane was formerly a muleteer, and a native of the city] . . .

"[Throughout] all this kingdom of Lara the land is very rough, and with cruel mountains, and with heaps of pebbles, and without grass or trees. But between them [the mountains], the valleys have palm trees, and wells of water and cisterns of rain water. They raise mares, and horses, which is the principal trade they have and they carry [them] to Ormuz, and from there to India. It is [a] very hot land in the summer but not as hot as Ormuz. It rains only a few times. They have winter and summer as here in Europe. Near this city, in a small mountain range, some animals breed which are the size of great roes, which give origin to a stone in the stomach, which they call *Bazar*, which is greatly valued among them, and much esteemed, since it is an antidote against poison.[*] This stone originates in those animals because of a grass they eat, which is not found in other parts. The stone is dark green in color, and so great and long as the little finger of a man, and I saw its experiment."

---

* Famous in the Middle Ages and in the Renaissance as an antidote against poison, the strange properties and effects of the bezoar stone are noted by the Portuguese doctors Amatus Lusitanus, *In Dioscoridis Anazarbei de Medica Materia Libros Quinque Enarrationes Eruditissimae*, Venice, 1553, p. 186-188 and Garcia da Orta, *Coloquios dos Simples, e Drogas he Cousas Mediçinais da India*, Goa, 1563 in Coloquio 45, and 58, and more particularly, and with great erudition, by the Spanish physician Doctor Niculoso de Monardes, *Dos Libros*, Seville, 1565 with abundant praise for its efficacy against swoons, worms and poisons. The English physician Frederick Slare, *Experiments and Observations upon Oriental and Other Bezoar-Stones*, London, 1715 seeks to discredit the bezoar stone amongst his contemporaries. Modern medicine has condemned the bezoar stone, crucified the old conjectures, and laid its supposed virtue to rest. But the modern mind, in worship of itself and the fleeting world of its creation, holds much in contempt that ignorance and vanity, shrouded in Mathematics, effect to despise as superstition. Our princes of the laboratories and experimental technique only cherish what they can measure or compute. But sirs! How can so many Hispanics, and others, who claim to have seen and tested its effect, been deceived about the bezoar stone? Please disabuse.

Itinerario de Antonio Tenreiro,
Capitulo III

CHAPTER XII

DESCRIPTION OF THE CITY OF SHIRAZ BY ANTONIO TENREIRO

"This city [of Shiraz] is great and head of the kingdom [and province of Fars], situated near a mountain range that is towards the west. It is very ancient, enclosed by [a] wall of stone, knocked down in many places. It has many inhabitants [thirty-five hundred in 1515 according to Gil Simões], with good houses, and most have panes of glass in windows, because it is very cold in the winter. It is very famous among the Moors in the kingdom of Persia, so much so that they say when Xiras [Shiraz] prospered Cairo was its suburb. The residents are Turkomans and Persians, white and people of fair complexion, with well proportioned bodies. They have difference in language because the Turks speak Turkish and the Persians speak Persian which is [a] sweeter language and better. They all wear cloth of linen, quilted in the winter, and with much cotton, and linings of rich skins, those who can afford them, because they are very costly in this land. The common people wear those of lambs and foxes. They wear *ceroulas*-draws, leggings and shoes bound at the soles with many *preguinhos*-small pieces of metal. They wear cloaks of *grā*-scarlet-in-grain, with blue and red cloths, which are worth much in this land. The land is well provided with meats, butter, wheat, barley, rice and saffron, and the land yields all these. They have many gardens and flower gardens (*ortas, e jardins*) in which there are good garden greens, and likewise apples, pears, peaches, quinces, grapes of Alicante, and in much greater abundance, doubled red roses, from which they make much rosewater, and of the fruit conserves, with which they trade at Ormuz. They raise many horses in the land, with which they likewise trade in India.

"In this land I entered a flower garden, which was of the past kings, that had [an] enclosure of two leagues, and in it I saw things of admiration principally some palaces constructed of marble, and of some stones, with excellent panes of glass, and very perfectly sculptured, and finished with plaster and very fine glazed tiles made in the land; groves of trees of all kinds, as in Hispania, all placed in rows, and put to the cord; cypress trees, very close, and very great, placed in two orders with [a] path between them, so that at noon it appears to be night, and so dark, that I feared to enter inside. They gather so many roses in this garden, when their time has come, that each day it exceeds twelve thousand pounds. In the middle of it is a great tank of water, and in the middle of the tank a very elegantly sculptured house which the lord of that land arranged to build for his diversion. And the Sufi [Shah Ismael], when he was in this city, went to this

81

house to enjoy himself, and to drink much wine, which for them is a thing of great delight, with some Moorish lords and captains, who passed to the said house with him in a small bark, and ate and drank with him; afterwards he ordered them to swim and to fight in the said tank, and some of them drowned, from which [fight or drowning?] he derived much pleasure and enjoyment."

Itinerario de Antonio Tenreiro,
Capitulo VI

CHAPTER XIII

DESCRIPTION OF A HUNT OF XEQUE ISMAEL, IN WHICH FERNAM GOMES DE LEMOS PARTICIPATED, BY GIL SIMOENS—1515

"And on Sunday [September 9, 1515] Xeque Ismael went to the hunt, and he carried the greater part of the people of the *arraial*-encampment [with him], and he arranged to enclose three or four leagues of very rough land in very high mountain ranges [near Maragoa, which we identify with the Persian city of Maragheh], and beating the bush they found themselves amidst much game, and they forced it to gather in a very great field, and the people surrounded it [the game] in such a manner that it remained entirely placed in a corral, and then he sent to call the ambassador [Fernão Gomes de Lemos], and as soon as he arrived with his people, the Xeque entered the enclosure.

"And inside were as many as one thousand and five hundred heads of wild animals, *a saber*, deer, gazelle, rams, buckgoats and wild goats and bears, jackals, wolves, and pigs. The king entered with a bow in hand, and his arrows commenced to fly, and each shot passed through three of these animals,[*] and after slaying many, and fatigued [by use] of the bow, he took a *treçado*-broad sword and commenced to slash at them, and he gave [a] blow which cleft an animal from head to tail, in such a manner that one part fell to one side, and the other part to the other side, and thus he cleft others across, and after he grew weary Dormiscão [Durmish Khan Shamlu] his companion, and the governor, and the captain of the guard, entered. Notwithstanding their great exertions, they did not deliver such great blows as the Xeque, and these finished slaying all the game.

"These things having terminated, they brought drink to the Xeque, and cucumber and blackberries, and he ordered drink to be given to the ambassador, and asked him if the king our lord hunted in such a manner, and then the Xeque related to him that during one winter he killed twenty thousand head at Sau [Saveh?] and during another winter fifty-two thousand head at Espão[†] [Isfahan]. After the king dispatched all the game to the *arraial*, he rode upon a horse, and rode a league

---

* *e de cada tiro pasava tres alimarias destas.* The fact seems scarcely credible. A variant reading: "and with each shot three of these animals passed" is conceivable, but not, I believe, intended by the author.

† Espaur in the Manuscript of Ajuda.

from that place to fish with a net that he threw with his own hand."

Cartas de Affonso de Albuquerque, Tomo II, Lisbon, 1898, p. 241: the manuscript of Vimieiro.

Codice 50-V-21 of the Biblioteca da Ajuda, Lisbon.

CHAPTER XIV

DESCRIPTION OF THE CITY OF TABRIZ BY ANTONIO TENREIRO

"Tabriz is [a] very great city situated towards the side of the west between two mountain ranges, which go widening, each one for its part, *a saber*, one for the part of the north, and [the] other for that of the south. It is flat and without [a] wall, with very noble houses of stone and mortar, with French walls (*taypas francesas*), all of one story or more, and with arched roofs. They have few windows, only apertures, which give light, because the land is very cold. They have very rich panes of glass in them, with many loops of colors and paintings. The houses, [those] which have great gardens and orchards, have very great and ancient edifices inside. It is very crowded in places, where there are gates of entrance and departure, which make it [Tabriz] stronger than [a] wall. It has many mosques and very high *alcorões*-minarets of masonry and cut rock, [a] thing of admiration. There are many large public squares covered above, in which the merchants reside and contract their business, because it has great trade. It has ten or twelve very great and well worked lodgings, and each one is a villa, where the merchants take quarters with their merchandise, and it has only one portal by which they enter, that has a thick chain across, forbidding access to any man on horse. And besides these, in which the merchants reside, there are many others for muleteers and their animals. It has many well-provided roads of all the trades.

"A very large enclosure is to one side of this city, with great orchards and gardens, where the houses of the Sufi are situated, and they are some very well made palaces constructed of very fine alabaster or marble of that land and with many very noble panes of glass. Around the said enclosure are numerous and very high poplar trees placed in order, and in places, very large and well cut tanks of water in which swans and birds of divers manners swim.

"This city is inhabited by Persians and some Turkomans, white people, and beautiful of face and person. They make a good impression and dress in satins, from which they make their quilted garments, and [with] cloths of *graā*-scarlet-in-grain in their cloaks, with many and rich *alamares*-frogs of gold, and with silk, and with very noble linings, which are worth much in this land. And the merchants of Russia, and thus of Venice and Turkey come here to merchandise.

"This city has many houses of bath wrought in elegant style, where they bathe in the winter and in the summer, which makes the people very white and very delicate. The

85

women are very beautiful and bear themselves well, and on occasion the honored ladies depart from their houses, and when they depart, they ride horseback on the best horses which they have. They sit in the saddle as the men do. Their garments are very tight through the sleeves, and embroidered on the arms, fitted to the body, and they reach to the foot, [and] open in front from the breasts to the waist, and thus even the blouses; and underneath draws of silk worked in gold and seed-pearls on the front side, over which they suit leggings of scarlet or purple-red cloth, with very delicate little shoes of silk and of leather. Over these garments they wear some upper garments fitted with tight and long sleeves, which hang free. They are lined with ermine and marten and with other linings. On the head [they wear] some *trançados*-braids with *rebuço*-covering; and this is the dress of all the women of the Sufi, and thus of other great lords and rich merchants. The common people wear fine quilted linens of colors, with cloaks of cloths of London, and other cloths, all with linings of fox and lamb, because one is not able to suffer the land without them, since it is very cold in the winter, as here in Hispania.

"The principal trade of this land, and [that] which renders the most to the Sufi, is from raw silk, which enters this city from other kingdoms of the Sufi, and from here they carry it to Turkey and other lands of [the] Moors and Christians. It is very well provided with *mantimentos*-provisions of all kinds: *a saber*, wheat, barley, rice, and many meats, and all at little cost; only firewood and coal are expensive, because they come from afar. One camel load in that city is worth six or seven *xays*, which is a coin of silver, each one being valued at a *tostão*. Two nations of Christians inhabit this place, and a good number of them live in the land [of Azerbaijan]; and some of them, whom they call Franks, have our customs and faith, and the majority of them are farmers and craftsmen of [the] mechanical art[s]. And [the] others are Armenians, most of whom are great merchants, and others make wine by trade and sell it secretly to the Moors. They have small churches and chapels in the said city where they say Masses, and they celebrate the divine offices to the manner of the primitive church, albeit with much fear.

"A river of very good water flows through the middle of this city, which serves it, and all the people drink it, and it is conveyed by conduits through all the roads beneath the ground; hence it falls that each road has some *bocays*-nozzles and locks of stone in certain places whence they tap it when they have need. It comes hot in the winter, and when it comes to the surface, in a little space it turns to ice. And during the summer this land is so hot, that [the] men, who trade in this,

86

are accustomed to preserve the ice in certain houses beneath the ground, and they sell *eruas*-vegetables to the common people in all the public squares; and the honored and rich people arrange to have snow fetched from the mountains, and they store it in their places, and they place it in water that they drink."

Itinerario de Antonio Tenreiro,
Capitulo XV

A LIST OF THE PRESENTS CARRIED BY FERNAM GOMES DE LEMOS TO XEQUE ISMAEL, IN 1515, ACCORDING TO AN *INSTRUMENTO* OR *MANDADO* OF AFONSO DE ALBUQUERQUE

Dated Ormuz, 5th May 1515

"Manuel da Costa factor of Ormuz, scriveners of the said factory, the captain-general, etc.: By this [instrument] I order you to deliver to Gil Simões, scrivener of the embassy which I send to Xeque Ismael by Fernão Gomes de Lemos and João de Sousa, second person, these things following and named; *a saber*, two bracelets of gold, one of them furnished with seven rubies, one being very large and six middle-sized ones, and containing twenty-nine diamonds, and [the] other [a] smaller bracelet with a great cat's eye and two middle-sized rubies and twenty-three small rubies around it, and with seventy-one diamonds of small size, and with three middle-sized emeralds and six small ones. The gold of the said bracelets weighed four marks [one mark equals eight ounces] at two hundred and fifty-six cruzados. And four rings of gold dyed in indigo, *a saber*, three with three great rubies in perfection, and another with a sapphire and twenty-seven rubies around it, the gold being worth fourteen cruzados, and furthermore a necklace (*joya de pescoço*) with a great ruby in the middle of it to the mode of the rings and with four middle-sized rubies and eight small ones and with two turquoises and with three pearls of [the] form of *perilha* [i.e. pear-shaped], a very great one and two of middle size, and a pear of amber ornamented in gold, and rubies, with one hundred rubies and sixty small diamonds, and with a chain of gold worth seventeen and one quarter cruzados. And thus you will deliver to him a *carapuça*-cap of black velvet ornamented with gold and rubies; the said *carapuça* has one hundred and eighty-one rubies and the gold is worth seventy-four cruzados, and thus you will deliver this money which I send to show to Xeque Ismael, *a saber*, five *Portuguezes* in *Portugezes* [sic] of gold and five *cruzados* in *cruzados* and five *Catolicos* and five *Manues* of gold and five *tostões* of silver, and thus you will deliver to him the sword ornamented in gold and [a] dagger worked in gold, and thus the lances ornamented in gold, and all the arms, thus cuirasses and *escarcellas*-game-bags and non-fire arms, and thus you will deliver to him three *bestas*-crossbows and six muskets with all their *almasem*-magazine and *atabio*-embellishments, *a saber*, one must understand in the arms which do not fire, an entire body of non-fire arms, and thus it shall be entirely accomplished without doubt, and by this and [with] your knowledge and [the] assent of the said scriveners, all will be carried into account: made in Ormuz on the 5th of May, Fernão Pimentel made it, of one thousand and five hundred and fifteen. The said items I order to be delivered to him to carry as presents to Xeque Ismael. Done on the said day, month and year. And furthermore you will deliver to him another *besta*-crossbow with its *almasem*. Done on the said day, month and year."

(Signed) Affonso de Albuquerque.
Cartas de Affonso de Albuquerque, Tomo II,
Lisbon, 1898., pgs. 149, 150

The copies of the manuscript of Gil Simões list the gifts carried by Fernão Gomes de Lemos to the court of the king of Persia. From those copies, aiming at completeness, we add to the list of the governor of India, the following:

"Item, thirty quintals of pepper.

Item, one quintal of cardamon.

Item, twenty quintals of ginger.

Item, ten quintals of tin.

Item, ten quintals of clove.

Item, ten quintals of copper.

Item, five quintals of cinnamon.

Item, two *faraçolas* [one *faraçola* equals ca. 18 Portuguese pounds] of benjamin.

Item, twenty quintals of sugar.

Item, six hundred [or six] pieces of *beatilhas*-fine muslin."

> *Cartas de Affonso de Albuquerque*, Tomo I, Lisbon, 1884, p. 392: the manuscript of Alcobaça.
>
> *Cartas de Affonso de Albuquerque*, Tomo II, Lisbon, 1898, p. 235: the manuscript of Vimieiro.

APPENDIX II

LETTER OF AFONSO DE ALBUQUERQUE TO XEQUE ISMAEL CONVEYED BY FERNAM GOMES DE LEMOS

"Xeque Ismael very great and powerful lord amongst the Moors. Afonso de Albuquerque, captain-major and governor of the Indies for the very high and very powerful King Dom Manuel, King of Portugal and of the Algarves, on this side and that side [of the] sea in Africa, lord of Guinea and of the conquest, the navigation and commerce of Ethiopia, Arabia, Persia and of India, and of the Kingdom and lordship of Ormuz and of the Kingdom and lordship of Goa: I inform you, how, gaining I the city and Kingdom of Goa, I found your ambassador in it, to whom I made great honor and I dealt with as [an] ambassador of such [a] great King and lord and I eyed all your things as if he had been dispatched to these parts for the King our lord. And because I am certain that the King our lord will be pleased to have knowledge, friendship and diplomatic relations with you, he has sent this messenger to you, by name Fernão Gomes de Lemos, *homem fidalguo*, [a] *criado*-servant of the King our lord, [a] man instructed in arms to our use and educated in war, who, I believe, will give to you good account of all things of war according to our usage, of the arms and horses of the King our lord, of his conquests and of the land he has conquered from the Moors, of the wealth and riches of his Kingdoms, of how powerful he is by sea and land, and of his armadas, how they enclose the seas of India and Constantinople and the greater sea[*] which march with your kingdoms and dominions, where the *naos* of the Kingdom of Portugal, which the King our lord sends each year, are always found.

"You well know how I conquered the City and Kingdom of Ormuz by order of the King our lord, and thenceforth I worked to have knowledge of your state, command and power, and I would have dispatched messengers to you if the things of Ormuz had not been damaged, which I expect in God will soon be settled, because I intend to go there in person, and thence I will work to see you along the littoral of the sea and ports of your Kingdoms; because the power which I bring in *naos* and people of the King our lord is on the sea to expel and destroy the *naos* of the sultan [of Egypt] that enter India and wish to remain there. This has been accomplished with [the] help of God, because his captain and armada were overthrown at Diu, and we seized all the *naos* and killed all his people, and later, in the city of Goa, I defeated and expelled them and conquered the city and their entire armada, as your ambassador will say to you. And be-

---

* Lit. *o mar mayor.*

90

cause I have known that he is your enemy, and makes war to you, I send this news to you, and offer you my person, people and armada of the King our lord against him, to assist in his destruction, and to be against him each time you petition me, because although you have the vastness of your Kingdoms, wealth and multitude of people, horses and arms, the sultan has the Red Sea of this side of India, and on the side of the Eastern Mediterranean (*mar de levamte*) he has Alexandria, and its sea, where he makes *naos*; and if you desire to destroy him by land, you will have great aid by sea from the armada of the King our lord, and I believe you will conquer his Kingdom and city of Cairo, and all his land and dominions, with very little effort. And thus the King our lord will render you great assistance by sea against the Turk, in such a manner [only] by great efforts will he be able to save himself, and being overthrown by the King our lord at sea and by you with your cavalry and great power on land, since you confine with him and have war with his peoples and lands, [this task will be accomplished*]. In the Indian Ocean (*mar da India*) the King our lord dispatches great armadas, by means of which he will be able to help you through the strait of Meca as far as Soyça [Suez] and the Toro [El Tur], which are very near to Cairo.

"Thus you should desire to have the friendship and favor of such a great King as the King our lord by sea and by land and to dispatch your ambassadors to him, and they may go by Constantinople or by Ormuz and they will be well received, and the King our lord will be pleased to know how far your Kingdoms and lordships extend; and if God wills that you make this concert and friendship, coming with your power upon the city of Cairo and lands of the great sultan that march with you, the King our lord with all his power will pass to Jerusalem and subdue all the land of that side, and of necessity the sultan will lose his state. Hence it is desirable for your messengers to be dispatched with your will and determination so that your desire in this business will be understood, and by them you will thus have Reply from the King our lord of his wishes in this deed. And meanwhile I shall be informed of your desires, or to what part the armada of the King our lord should arrive in order to make the greatest damage and destruction to the land of the sultan."

Cartas de Affonso de Albuquerque, Tomo I, Lisbon, 1884, pgs. 387-389 Codice 50-V-21 of the Biblioteca da Ajuda, folhas 135, 136

---

* The sentence is incomplete, and a phrase of this, or similar import, is necessary to complete the meaning.

APPENDIX III

THE INSTRUCTION (or *REGIMENTO*) WHICH AFONSO DE ALBU-
QUERQUE GAVE TO FERNAM GOMES DE LEMOS AND GIL SIMOENS
OF WHAT THEY SHOULD SAY AND DO IN THEIR EMBASSY TO
PERSIA

"This is the manner and *Regimento* which you Fernão
Gomes de Lemos will have in your going and coming to
where I now send you for service of God and of the King
our lord, and you Gil Simões for scrivener of the embassy, the
following:

"Item. Your going will be by whatever mode and manner
that you will be able [to go] directly to where Xeque Ismael
is, to whom with all reverence and respect you will make that
reverence which is due to such a great King.

"Item. Arriving at Ormuz, you will ask Coje Atar [Khwaja
Attar] to arrange to give you four mounts for your persons
and for those who go with you, and for the other things for
your expense and despatch of your voyage which you carry
by my letters.

"Item. In your journey which you make, you will always be
at the order, counsel and determination of Braim Benate
[Ibrahim *Benate*], his ambassador, not buying anything without him, and [without] his permission, nor provisions for
your needs, nor will you separate from him to go to see cities,
squares, places, roads, fetes [or] games, nor another way save
what he makes; all will be by his order, because you well know
how the Moors naturally desire to make all [the] damage
they can to us.

"Item. You will say to Xeque Ismael from my part that I
send to visit him by the greatness of his fame, dominion and
spirit, and for the goodness and greatness of such a prince,
and because he protects Christians and honors and favors
them.

"Item. You will say to him how the King our lord would
be pleased to have knowledge and friendship with him, and
that he will assist him in the war against the sultan [of
Egypt], and his destruction, and that I, in his name and
from his part offer him [the] armada, people and artillery
that I bring, and the fortresses, places and dominions that
he has in India.

"Item. You will know of the Christians of those parts, if
they have [the] oratory of our faith and truly believe that
Our Lord was born of [the] Virgin Mary, Our Lady, died and
suffered on [the] cross for our salvation and arose on the
third day.

92

"Item. Furthermore you will see if you will be able to bring with you some of these Christians differing in some thing of our faith, or prescribe how they should go to Rome, although it would be better to go by way of Portugal.

"Item. You will see their Churches, ornaments and their altars, images of saints, and if they have Our Lord on the cross and the image of Our Lady; and thus the clergy and friars, and the mode of their life and dress; and thus of some bodies of saints, martyrs [and] apostles, if their bodies lie in these parts.

"Item. I order you to be loyal to the particulars [of] this *Regimento*, and both of you to conform to it, and thus the interpreter, so as to avoid difference of accounts, and when you touch upon some things of those which they ask you of Portugal, you will know how to say them without contradiction, and they will find you in all truth."

> *Cartas de Affonso de Albuquerque*, Tomo I, Lisbon, 1884, pgs. 389, 390
> Codice 50-V-21 of the Biblioteca da Ajuda, folha 137

APPENDIX IV

LETTER OF FERNAM GOMES DE LEMOS TO THE KING D. MANUEL PORTUGUESE TEXT

Senhor—porque meus dessejos foy sempre Morrer em cousas dacreçemtamento de vosso Real estado açeytey a embayxada que a° dalbuquerque mamdou ao xeques mael pomdo me diamte o seruyço que nyso fazya a vosalteza em thomaar este camynho o quaall foy asaz trabalhosso como lla pode ser emformaado pelo lyuro que lhe vaay da dita embayxada asy por ser llomgo como por ser terra nam sabyda. E asy pela thomada durmuz de que ho xeques mael nam foy muyto contemte pela qual vyajem lleyxey huũa naão de duzemtos thones pela esperamça que me o capitam moor deu de me serem galardoados meus seruyços depois de mynha vymda ho achey faleçido E eu com detrimjnaçam de hyr daar conta a vosalteza do que lla pasey ouue llopo Soarez por voso seruyço ficaar eu ca homde ho seruyrey nesta yda que prazemdo a nosso Senhor se fara e acabara o que vossalteza deseja E desejamos aqueles que em vosso seruyço caa amdam. stprita em cochim a iiij dias de Janeyro de 1517

> (*assinado*) Fernam Gomes de Llemos
> Torre do Tombo, Corpo Cronológico,
> Parte 1ª Maço 21 Documento 4

APPENDIX V

LETTER OF JOAM DE MEIRA TO THE KING D. MANUEL
PORTUGUESE TEXT

Senhor—Eu crero que nom espreuy ysto a vosa alteza nũa
carta que ho quapytam mor dom duarte me dyse que lhe dese
pera hyr com as suas ha quall he de sete folhas espryta de
berbo ha berbo e leua seys selos tres nuũ quabo e tres no
outro na quall dou mjuda conta a vosa alteza de tudo ho que
me tem mandado haçerqua das quartas que vosa alteza mandou ha ellRey de Bacora e acerqua de mjll e dozentos leques
que elle mandou prometer ha Dyego lopez de sequeyra voso
quapytam mor por bayRem e quatyfa fyqando elle vasalo de
vosa alteza e asy mujtas outras cousas que nela vam que sam
voso serujço dygo senhor que baçoRa se fez muj grande cousa
do tempo que hi descubry a este qabo e a causa senhor por
que he por terremos trauto nele/ porque acode agora de todo

fol 1v   o mundo haly ha gente asy a bosquar ha especyarya como
anjs e Roupa de canbaya eu Senhor fuy ter a bacora ha qujnze
dyas do mes dagosto de qujnhentos vynte e hũ anos e achey
tanta pymenta neste luguar nas maos dos mouros que valya
ha quoRenta e ojto pardaos ho baar ha qall elles tynham
comprada daqele tempo que vosa alteza dava qyntaes pera
Ormuz handava ho estrejto muj cheo dela e por yso estava tam
bayxa e nom tardou muytos dias que nom veo hũa quafelea
de terra de xama que heram setecentos quamellos e outra
cousa nom trazyam senom ouro em baras moeda amoedada
contas mujto fynas mujtos vjludos e veos mujtos enfyndos
chamalotes e acafram e pa*pele*[?] de mao e outras muytas
mercadorjas que eu ya vy em purtugal e muito azougue
enfyndo ha pymenta Senhor saltou logo a setenta e depos
esta quarfel*ea*[?] nom tardou muito que nom veo outra de
qujnhentos quamelos preguntej a el Rey se sohya de vjr a
hahy cada hũ anno tamanha qafla djse me que nom djse me
que esta quafla estava pera hyr pera aden e daden hyr ter a
quambaya por que quada anno fazya seu quamjnho per aden
e que aden/ lhe espreuera que nom fose porque estavamos

fol 2r   de guera com quambaya e que nom podjam pasar la asj que
esta Rezam Senhor lhe fez hyrem antes aquelle outro estrejto
que nom ho daden sam dezasejs djas de jornada de sama a
bacora e hasy Senhor que hos mercadores me dyseram que
por esta quausa vyeram ter aquele estrejto e por nom acharem
Senhor tanta espycyarya como avyam mester se vyeram mujtos deles ha ormuz pera vender suas mercadoryas y comprarem
pymenta pera se tornarem e qujs sua mofyna que todas suas
fazendas tjnham dentro nalefandegua quando foy aquela
trjçam parece me Senhor que tudo perderyam deyxo Senhor
ysto dygo que segundo vou entendendo desta Jndea que vosa

alteza tem majs nesesydade de hũ so homem que de homens
acuda lhe vosa alteza ho majs çedo que poder hũ homem antes
que com muitos homes porque hey muj gram medo que se va
tudo de Romarya segundo que vou enxergado e praza a deus
que seja eu mentyroso beyjarey as mãos de vosa alteza com-
endar me hũ alvara pera me hyr e ljcença pera des[?] escravos
que me servam noso Senhor acrecente os djas de uyda e estado
de vosa alteza de quochym vinte e hũ dias de Janejro de qujnhentos e vjnte e dous annos

    bejjo as mãos de vosa Real alteza

(*assinado*) Joam de Mejra
Torre do Tombo, Corpo Cronológico,
Parte 1ª Maço 27 Documento 97

TABLE OF CONTENTS

PART I

EMBASSIES, NAVIGATIONS AND PEREGRINATIONS

PART II

DESCRIPTIONS

APPENDIX

INDEX

INDEX

INDEX

INDEX

INDEX